Teaching with Caldecott Books

ACTIVITIES ACROSS THE CURRICULUM

By Christine Boardman Moen

SCHOLASTIC
PROFESSIONAL **B**OOKS

New York ◆ Toronto ◆ London ◆ Auckland ◆ Sydney

Cover Design by Vincent Ceci
Design by Kate Panzer

ISBN 0-590-49079-6

12 11 10 9 8 7 6 5 4 3 2   1 2 3 4 5/9

Printed in the U.S.A.

The term Caldecott/Caldecott Award and the reproduction of the facsimile of the Caldecott Medal are used with permission of the American Library Association.

This book
is lovingly dedicated
to my family:
Alex's hugs,
Ruth's smiles,
and Tom's belief in me.

Contents

Acknowledgments

I thank the following people, who helped me in ways both big and small: Jolene Soehl; Sue Camp; Jim O'Brien; Rochelle Murray and her staff at the Davenport Public Library; the staff and administration of Blue Grass Elementary School in Blue Grass, Iowa; the Bi-State Literacy Council; Diane Wirtz; Betty Frasier; Hallie Still-Caris; and last but not least, my mother, who called all my relatives and told them about this book and watched my children while I wrote the final manuscript.

Introduction

In *Caldecott & Co.: Notes on Books & Pictures*, Maurice Sendak describes the task of the illustrator as that of "quickening" or breathing life into the pictures of children's books.

The idea of quickening can also be applied to the children who read illustrated books. After all, children breathe life into books when they construct meaning from the text and pictures.

I won't go into all the reasons you should use Caldecott books in your classroom. All that is explained in Chapter 1. What I'd like to point out is that *Teaching with Caldecott Books: Activities Across the Curriculum* describes a whole language-critical thinking approach to teaching reading, writing, listening, speaking, and thinking using the Caldecotts as the literature base.

So go ahead. Use the Caldecotts and the approach described within these pages. I bet both will "quicken" your teaching, your classroom, your students, and, most of all, you!

Whole Language,
Whole Learning
with
Caldecott Books

Using the Caldecott collection of children's books either to begin to build the framework of your whole language instructional lesson plans or to enhance your existing plans is as natural as whole language itself. Why?

First, because the Caldecotts contain art that enhances each story. Whether it's John Steptoe's lushness, Maurice Sendak's playfulness, or Molly Bang's boldness, the art helps tell the story and create meaning. Thus, each story is "twice told"—an idea explained in Kenneth S. Goodman et al's *Language and Thinking in School: A Whole Language Curriculum*. Consequently, when students pick up a Caldecott children's book, they benefit from experiencing a story that's told twice through the unique blend of words and illustrations.

Secondly, the Caldecotts are a recognizable, ready-made source of literature that parents can identify with as "real" literature. This in turn may help ease some parents' uneasiness about their child's move from the basal to children's literature for language instruction. In addition, within the Caldecott collection a variety of ethnic groups are well represented, and this representation is especially important in our ever-changing multicultural schools.

Finally, the books in the Caldecott collection provide a variety of unique language experiences. Many contain the necessary repetition and predictability to enhance students' language-learning experiences. At the same time, students may find the variety of text lengths appealing; some stories can be devoured as a quick snack while others are more of a feast!

Caldecott Books in Later Chapters

Blueberries for Sal	*A Chair for My Mother*
Crow Boy	*Freight Train*
Frog and Toad Are Friends	*Jumanji*
Lon Po Po	*Make Way for Ducklings*
On Market Street	*Ox-Cart Man*
The Snowy Day	*Strega Nona*
Truck	*Where the Wild Things Are*
Why Mosquitoes Buzz in People's Ears	

In this book 15 Caldecott books model specific instructional strategies, critical thinking strategies, and extended language activities. However, at the end of each language activity, additional Caldecotts are suggested for use with that particular activity. In this way, you are encouraged to substitute another book in place of the one used or to develop a variety of your own activities.

The Caldecott books listed here are not grouped around themes. Themes can be a significant part of whole language classrooms, but they were purposely not used here, because the Caldecotts lend themselves to a number of different themes. It is more appropriate for you to develop themes that will satisfy not only the learning needs of your students but also your own specific instructional or curricular goals.

The Goal of Whole Language Instruction

The goal of whole language instruction is to support, encourage, and create literate, confident, responsible learners—whole children who are not word-bound, hesitant readers, writers, and thinkers with poor self-images. At the same time, whole language instruction attempts to use each student's prior knowledge to help create meaning.

Integration Is the Key

With whole language instruction, every language event that requires students to read, write, speak, listen, or think influences future language events. In this way, students are always "in the process" of becoming literate.

In addition, whole language instruction promotes the idea that reading is transactional, so each student negotiates meaning. Consequently, language learning takes place as a result of approximations as each student uses language to meet his or her individual purposes and needs. And because language learning becomes a series of approximations, students learn to become risktakers and not to fear making mistakes.

Whole language also demands that teachers integrate the language

processes and avoid isolating them into units, time allotments, or subjects thereby keeping the richness of context intact. In this way, language processes naturally stay together—and when you think about it, it's much harder to separate language processes than it is to keep them together!

Most important, whole language instruction fosters language ownership by capitalizing on what Ken Goodman calls in *What's Whole in Whole Language?* "authentic literacy events." For example, given a test of spelling words isolated on a list, many students can get 100 percent correct but cannot transfer those same conventional spellings when writing a paragraph. Why does this happen?

Because the words were not learned while engaged in authentic (and meaningful) literacy events, the students often do not assume ownership of the words. In other words, students who must learn isolated spelling words from lists don't have the benefit of "encounters." The more often a student encounters a word while reading, listening, speaking, thinking, and writing and uses the word to meet literacy needs, the more likely the student will assume ownership of the word and use it purposefully.

The Variety of Materials

Because whole language instruction integrates the language processes of reading, writing, speaking, listening, and thinking, it utilizes a variety of instructional materials. These materials help extend each student's language experiences beyond literature to include the language materials of everyday life.

For example, in addition to using the Caldecotts as a part of the literature base within the classroom, students also use newspapers, magazines, maps, reference books, calendars, phone books, cookbooks, brochures, schedules, catalogs, signs, posters, packages, and labels. Each type of instructional material requires students to apply language in a different way, because each of the materials has unique features—a cookbook is unlike a newspaper, a map is unlike a calendar, yet each can be used for language experiences that help students expand their own language usage.

Instructional Strategies

An instructional strategy is the framework for language activities that extend students' language experiences beyond reading the text of a book. In other words, strategies are where the learner and the learning meet.

The main purpose of any instructional strategy, regardless of where its emphasis lies, is to facilitate the integration of all of the language processes. Although a strategy may be identified as an authorship strategy, its intent is to weave all of the language processes together during an extended language experience that focuses on writing.

A variety of instructional strategies as well as language-extension activities are discussed in Chapter 2. One important note, however: It's important for you to select those strategies that are consistent with your teaching style, your students' needs, and your philosophy of whole language instruction, regardless of what other whole language teachers do.

The Bonuses of Whole Language Instruction

Learning that can't be labeled simply language arts will start to occur in your whole language classroom. This "Learning Across the Curriculum" is a natural result of language instruction that involves reading maps, computing shipping costs on catalog orders, and inspecting food labels for chemical additives.

In addition, because student conferencing is encouraged, students spend more time engaged in language learning from and with each other than they do waiting for the teacher to show them the "correct way" or to "give the right answer."

Finally, whole language instruction is the perfect setting for students to develop and use critical thinking. Because students involve themselves in entire pieces of literature as well as other authentic literacy resources, the demands to think critically are much greater than those required to complete isolated-skill worksheets.

Some Final Words About Whole Language Instruction

The information provided to this point is probably a starting point for some of you and a refresher for others. Certainly it is a starting point if you are now beginning to move toward whole language instruction. If that is the case, you may wish to read some of the excellent books listed in the bibliography. Several offer unique, satisfying descriptions of whole language instruction.

If, however, you're an old hand at whole language instruction (anyone with at least a semester under his or her belt qualifies), you are already familiar with many of the ideas presented in this chapter and can smile comfortably and feel reassured that you are on the right track.

Finally, I'd like to share some observations about whole language classrooms. See if you agree with me. Whole language classrooms promote:

◆ The use of good children's literature as well as other authentic literacy resources to enhance and extend students' language experiences

◆ A supportive environment that allows students to take risks and make mistakes that lead to language learning

◆ The use of a variety of instructional strategies that integrate reading, writing, speaking, listening, and thinking

Whole language classrooms avoid:

◆ Round-robin read-aloud groups that trap students into falsely judging their reading abilities and set students up for humiliating exercises in "gotcha"

◆ Worksheets that break language into skill areas that destroy the naturalness of using reading, writing, speaking, listening, and thinking together to create language meaning

◆ Literature with strictly controlled vocabularies in which the richness of language has been stripped to make the stories more understandable according to predetermined ability levels

Instructional Strategies: Where Learner and Learning Meet

An instructional strategy is a way of organizing instruction to facilitate learning. In other words, it's where the learner and learning meet. Eight strategies are described in this chapter: authorship, cooperative learning, games, comprehension, story structure, listening lab, performing arts, and visual arts. Critical thinking is treated separately, in Chapter 4.

The purpose of instructional strategies, of course, is to promote the integration of the language processes: reading, writing, speaking, listening, and thinking. And although strategies organize instruction, they do not restrict it, because strategies are often blended. To take it one step further, you can think of strategies as "learning ingredients."

Try this recipe for learning in your classroom:

Take one bouncy, lively book, add a game of sentence building, stir in some authorship (perhaps a letter-writing activity), sprinkle heavily with critical-thinking questions, and top it off with visual art—a beautifully illustrated student-made poster! Sounds like a lot more fun than worksheets, doesn't it?

From this point in Chapter 2, each strategy is described and language-extension activities are illustrated to give you an overview of the strategies as well as to provide you with additional activities using a wide variety of Caldecotts. Many strategies and language-extension activities are also described in detail and used in a number of different ways in Chapters 5 to 11.

Authorship Strategy

The authorship strategy uses writing as the basis for all of its language-extension activities. Writing often gets pushed aside in the classroom because it takes time and a great deal of energy. However, many whole language teachers agree that students should be allowed to write for at least a half hour each day.

If you feel that you can't devote a half hour each day to writing, let me try to persuade you by pointing out that writing nurtures many critical-thinking skills. Students think critically when they plan their written communication, organize ideas, classify those ideas, judge and

select them for inclusion in their writing, sequence their ideas, and, finally, apply the principles of good writing. All this from just one writing experience!

Writing, like thinking, is NOT something taught when students finally reach the upper grades. Using invented spelling and given the opportunity to read his or her writing to an adult, every student (even a kindergartner) can be a writer worthy of expressing himself or herself. After all, if students don't practice writing on a daily basis, how will they ever learn to write?

STUDENT JOURNALS

Journals help teachers get to know their students better, because students fill them with writing and drawing based on self-selected topics. At the same time, journals allow students the freedom to write without risk. Reactions to books, plays, and school activities, as well as personal narratives, are frequent topics for journal writing.

CHARACTER DIARIES

Another twist to the student journal is the character diary. Students pretend they are a character and write diary entries. This activity can be extended by encouraging note passing between student "characters." Simple student mailboxes placed in a corner of the classroom will assure that characters receive their mail.

For example, students pretending to be Max in *Where the Wild Things Are* might write a diary describing their lives on the island with their wild friends. Students may then wish to carry the role-playing further and write letters or notes to Max's mother. The letters could even be turned into a script for a Readers' Theater presentation (see page 38).

LEARNING LOGS

Learning logs are different from journals in that the learning recorded in the log is sometimes more spontaneous—"light-bulb learning," I call it. Students record "insights" when, for instance, they want to remember something for future reference or they finally understand the meaning of a word. Students may wish to share the information in their

logs during student conferencing time or to keep the log to themselves. Shared or not, a log is an excellent place to record words from the Wall of Words activity, which is described in detail in Chapter 3.

Finally, it's important to note that the learning log is an all-purpose record. The information recorded in it crosses all subject areas and includes insights from math and science as well as language arts.

LETTER WRITING

This language-extension activity gives students the opportunity to write a variety of letters. Students can assume the role of a character in a book. For example, students become Al in *Hey, Al* and write a letter home describing what it's like to have wings and fly.

Students can also write letters of advice, warning, congratulations, and sympathy to other characters in other books. For example, students write a letter of advice to Danny and Walter Budwing, characters in *Jumanji*, advising them to follow the directions of the game.

Or students can write letters to authors. Any replies are shared with the class and posted. (If several students write to the same author, you may wish to send the letters together with a cover letter of your own asking the author to write a single letter to the class. This may increase your chances of getting a response.) Also, you may wish to write to the author care of his or her publisher.

For example, after reading part or all of *Bill Peet: An Autobiography*, students may wish to read other books by the author-illustrator and write to him asking him what he does that helps him think of stories and illustrations.

WRITING BOOKS

Given opportunity and encouragement, students will write books about almost any topic imaginable. If you have avoided having students write books because of the hassles of publishing, just consider any piece of student writing "published" when it is read by anyone other than its author. If you expand your definition of *published* to include writing that has simply "gone public," it's easier to give your students more chances to write.

Student-created books can range from those written on lined paper stapled together with a construction-paper cover to more elaborate books with a cardboard cover and laminated pages. (*Classroom Strategies That Work: An Elementary Teacher's Guide to Process Writing*, by Nathan et al., is an excellent book that provides sound advice about publishing as well as managing a process-writing classroom.)

The main thing, however, is to get students to harness their vivid imaginations and natural storytelling abilities to get their ideas in written form—with illustrations, if possible. One good technique is group writing. Creating a book as a group not only fosters the strategy of cooperative learning but also helps students learn to think (and rethink) out loud.

Students have a variety of different story types to choose from. For example, they can write story sequels (stories that come after the endings of books they have read), such as a story about the mother's birthday party and her reaction to the girl's birthday gift after they've read *Mr. Rabbit and the Lovely Present*. Or they can write prequels (stories that come before), such as a story about Frog waking up in April, getting dressed, and walking to Toad's house after they've read "Spring" in *Frog and Toad Are Friends*. Another option is "equals" (stories that mirror a book's original format). For example, students could write a book entitled *Eskimo to Shawnee: The Peoples of the United States of America* after reading the Caldecott *Ashanti to Zulu: African Traditions*. (This is a good writing and social-studies learning opportunity.)

Of course, students can write original books too. Some ideas include alphabet books, rhyming books, books based on opposites, as well as acrostics, books with numbers and time, books with repetition, and, finally, "redone" Caldecotts, in which students change either the beginning, middle, or end of the book.

One final note: A list of books each student writes should be kept, as well as a list of books each student reads. Both lists are visible and positive signs of student growth.

BROCHURES

Walk into almost any store, business, or organization and you will

find brochures. Often schools send brochures home with students during Fire Safety Week and Library Week. Brochures contain a lot of information in a small amount of space. That makes them ideal communication pieces for students to model, because they require exact language. For example, after reading *A Tree Is Nice*, students can create a brochure that describes why trees are nice.

NEWSPAPERS

Newspaper articles and features used as models for writing activities add yet another dimension to students' language ownership. Once again, students choose from a variety of activities.

Students can write a news story based on an event that happened in a book. For example, they might write a story describing Blériot crossing the English Channel after they've read *The Glorious Flight: Across the Channel with Louis Blériot*.

In addition, students can write book reviews. After reading *Rumpelstiltskin* and *Duffy and the Devil*, students might compare and contrast the two story lines and tell which one they liked best and why. (A twist is to have students videotape their reviews or even debate their opinions before the camera.)

Students can write human-interest stories and character profiles. After reading *Saint George and the Dragon*, students might pretend to interview the Red Cross Knight and write an article entitled "What Makes a Hero." (This would be a great role-playing exercise too.)

Students can create an advertisement selling one of the books. After reading *The Talking Eggs*, students might create an advertisement such as "Buy *The Talking Eggs*, and find out why the yoke is really on Rose and her mother!"

BIOGRAPHIES AND AUTOBIOGRAPHIES

Students love to write about themselves and other people (even if these people are monsters and talking animals).

They can interview anyone—their teachers, parents, or relatives—and write short biographies. Or students can chronicle their own lives. For example, after reading *Bill Peet: An Autobiography*, they might write

(and illustrate) their own autobiographies.

CHARACTER PROFILES

Students learn to identify character traits by focusing on what characters say, what they do, and what others say about them or do to them. For instance, after examining characters using these areas as guidelines, students can then write sentences describing different characters. After reading *Many Moons*, they might write a sentence describing the kind of person the King is and another sentence describing the kind of person his daughter Lenore is.

POETRY

Every classroom should contain several books of poetry as well as tapes and records of poetry and songs. These are invaluable authentic literacy resources.

After examining the Caldecotts, you'll realize that several of them are really short poems with beautiful rhythm and imagery. You may want to encourage your students to model their writing after some of these poems, individually or as an exercise in group writing. For example, after reading *Ten, Nine, Eight*, students might create a poem based on the book's pattern. Here's an example:

> Ten turtles,
> Nine Nancy's,
> Eight crates to lift and pull.
> Seven Saucers,
> Six saddles,
>
> Five hives of bees that buzz.
> Four doors,
> Three trees,
> And two totes.
> But one—count ME,
> Only one of Me!

JOB BANKS

The purpose of the job bank is to develop students' curiosity, awareness, and understanding of different occupations and professions. Students can identify occupations and professions associated with any of the plots of the books. Examples include:

> farmer: *Owl Moon*
> janitor: *Hey, Al*
> surveyor: *The Little House*
> dance instructor: *Fables*
> teacher: *Crow Boy*
> hair designer: *Finders Keepers*
> train engineer: *Freight Train*

These occupations and professions can be listed and displayed on an ongoing basis in a "World of Work" display area. Students add information to the display, such as a newspaper photograph of a farmer or a dance-studio ad clipped from an old phone book's yellow pages. Students also add written information from reference materials to the display.

In addition, to provide students with opportunities to listen for information, to interview, and to write, guest speakers representing various occupations or professions can be scheduled to give students a firsthand account of what it's like to power a locomotive cross-country or to stand all day cutting and curling hair.

SYNECTICS

Synectics is an instructional strategy that was designed by William J.J. Gordon and his associates to develop "creativity groups" within industrial organizations. Today, however, more and more teachers are using synectics to help expand their students' creativity. Using this strategy, students "play" with comparisons or analogies and expand their thinking before writing or problem solving.

The following example is a modified version of synectics and is one I have used to introduce students to synectics.

Have each student respond in writing to the following questions as you ask each question aloud:

- How is school like a computer?
- Pretend you are the front door of your school. What do you hear, feel, see, and smell?
- How is school both light and dark?*

As a large group, have students share their responses as you record them on the board.

An example of using a Caldecott is:

After reading *Mufaro's Beautiful Daughters*, students respond to the following questions:

- Direct comparison: "How is the jungle forest like a blanket?"
- Personal comparison: "Pretend you are a monkey sitting in a tree in the jungle forest. What do you see, hear, smell, and feel?"
- Comparing conflict: "Give an example of a jungle forest city."

After this brainstorming session, students may wish to write their reaction to the story in their journal; write an original story of what it's like to be lost in a jungle forest at night; investigate plants and animals of Zimbabwe (the story's setting), paying particular attention to their descriptions; or read *Once a Mouse*... and compare and contrast its jungle forest and creatures with those found in *Mufaro's Beautiful Daughters*.

Using the words and ideas from the synectics exercise, have students in small groups or individually, write a telephone poem. (Pick a telephone number at random, such as 345-2662. The first line of the poem contains three words, the second line contains four words, and so forth.) When the poems are completed, have students read them aloud.

WALL OF WORDS

The Wall of Words is not only an authorship strategy but also a component built into the instructional model in Chapter 3, where a detailed example is provided. The Wall of Words has a multiple purpose:

---

*The last question in many synectic exercises is an oxymoron such as: "Describe something that runs slowly." However, using an additional comparison for the third question can also be effective.

to check each student's prior knowledge, to let students see their oral vocabulary words in written form, and to provide an accessible list of words from which students can "scrounge." (Students scrounge words when they copy them from charts, books, posters, or any other place to meet their writing needs.)

Cooperative-Learning Strategy

The cooperative-learning strategy is designed to put more teachers into every classroom by enlisting students' help. In other words, by encouraging students' participation and empowering them, you'll have more teachers in the classroom as students teach one another.

CONFERENCING

No one establishes a better case for the necessity and rewards of student-to-student conferencing, as well as student-to-teacher conferencing, than Brian Cambourne and Jan Turbill, in their book *Coping with Chaos*. (Turbill's books *No Better Way to Teach Writing!* and *Now We Want to Write!* are also excellent resources.) Students CAN learn from one another and support one another. Conferencing takes place when students ask one another questions, share one another's ideas, read one another's work, and work together to solve problems. Cooperation— NOT competition—is stressed. (Student conferencing is absolutely magnificent to watch and listen to!)

Students also conference with teachers in a variety of ways. For instance, a student-to-teacher conference can be informal, as when the teacher quickly stops and offers praise or answers a question. On the other hand, a student-to-teacher conference can be formal: A teacher may want to listen while a student reads aloud a page from the book he's currently reading, or she may want to help a student edit his written work by asking clarifying questions. Getting conferencing time to run smoothly and productively takes time and energy, but it will help meet the needs of your students as well as your need to evaluate student progress.

OLDER-YOUNGER READER PROGRAM

Some teachers use a reading-enhancement-and-recovery program in which upper-elementary students read books aloud to lower-elementary students. The program not only adds to the number of books each younger student interacts with but also reinforces the reading habit in older students who may be reluctant readers. Such cross-age reading programs have proven successful and are well worth implementing.

Games Strategy

Tell students they're going to play a game, and they immediately become enthusiastic about learning. And although I personally believe all the strategies and extension activities described in this book are enjoyable (I admit some prejudice here), this strategy may become slightly more popular than some others because of the following activities' gamelike nature.

ADOPT-A-WORD

This activity promotes REAL word ownership. Each student chooses a word from the Wall of Words and writes it on a card. The word is taped to the student's clothing or chair. Throughout the day, students ask each other their words. At the end of the day, students are encouraged to record their word (and others if they choose) in their learning logs if they feel they've "adopted" the word and it now lives with them.

Students may also choose to store their words in their own word bags or boxes. A periodic "cleaning" of the bags or boxes helps students claim words they still consider theirs, just as it helps students discard words they no longer feel they "own."

PUNCTUATION PUNCH-OUT

More fun than a worksheet, Punctuation Punch-Out helps students learn and practice punctuation exactly where punctuation is used—in a story!

The best time to do Punctuation Punch-Out is after students have

read and comprehended the story. (Try Punctuation Punch-Out after a shared group reading experience in which students respond to critical thinking questions and point out and explain the uses of various punctuation marks.)

To play Punctuation Punch-Out, follow these steps:

1. Word process the text of each page of the book. For example, text appears on 28 pages in *Blueberries for Sal*. Consequently, you should have 28 pages of word-processed text. (You are word processing the text to avoid destroying your individual student book copies. The student book copies will be needed later during the small-group activity.)

2. Nip out the punctuation marks with a paper punch. (Don't remove ALL the punctuation—just those marks you wish students to practice.)

3. Glue or tape the text pages to construction paper. Use different colors of construction paper to help facilitate student grouping. For example, with the 28 pages from *Blueberries for Sal*, glue the first four pages of text to red construction paper, the next four pages to blue, and so on. Dividing the pages using this color-coded method allows you to have seven student groups with four pages of text each.

4. Add a part of a self-checking message on labels on the back of each page. I place one word or punctuation mark on the back of each page of text: This is the self-checking part of the activity so when students turn the pages over, they will know if they are correct or not. (The message contains 28 separate words and marks—one for each page.)

5. Divide students into groups and give each group a story section. (The pages of each section should be scrambled. This way the Red Group gets text pages 1-4, the Blue Group gets pages 5-8, and so forth, but the pages are not in order within each story section.)

6. Explain to students that they have four consecutive pages of the book that are out of sequence. They are to follow these directions:

Each Student Group

a) reads the text pages and arranges them in order.

b) supplies the punctuation marks where the punctuation has been punched out (use pencils).

c) changes places with another group and checks that group's punctuation and story sequence using the book as a guide.

d) marks any errors the group has made using plastic winks, etc.

e) returns to its own story section and corrects any errors. Each group then checks its own work using the book as a guide.

7. Next, show students the self-checking message or code and ask students if their pages are sequenced correctly.

8. Ask the student group with the story's first four pages to begin reading the story aloud. The remaining groups listen and read their pages aloud when it's their turn.

9. Display the Punctuation Punch-Out pages along with student-created illustrations on a classroom or hall wall. Send students during SSR time to "read the writing on the wall!"

BLACK-OUT BLOCKS

This cloze-reading activity is an excellent way to get students to use syntactic and semantic language cues to construct meaning during the reading process. To prepare a passage for student use, you may wish to use the text copy from Punctuation Punch-Out and black out words with a marker. If you leave underlined spaces for deleted words, students will be able to see each word's length. In addition, you may choose to leave a beginning letter or blend as a helpful guide when doing this activity for the first time with your students. To complete the activity, students write the missing words above the blacked-out areas. In groups of two, students compare their words with the original text.

Black-out blocks can also be done as a group activity using the overhead projector. To do this, first cover words with masking tape. After students make their predictions, remove the tape to check for accuracy and meaning. Whenever a student has supplied a word that does not

match the text yet does not alter the meaning of the sentence, the two sentences are recorded on chart paper and shared with the class. Meaning, not word-for-word identification, is the focus.

There are several different ways to prepare a cloze-reading activity. You could delete every fifteenth word after the initial paragraph, delete all of the nouns or verbs, or delete all words with the long *i* sound. The more frequent the deletions, the more difficult this activity becomes; therefore, it's important not to make the deletions so close together that the activity frustrates students.

SENTENCE LINE-UP

The object of this game is to unscramble the words of a sentence and to line them up in a meaningful sentence. To prepare the game, copy sentences from the book the class is currently reading or one it has just completed onto oaktag strips and separate the words and individual punctuation marks. Next, put each sentence's words and punctuation marks into a big paper bag. To begin play, divide the students into groups according to the number of words and punctuation marks in the sentences you have chosen. For example, the following sentence from *Song and Dance Man* would require a group of 13 students for its nine words and four punctuation marks: "'Supper in an hour!' Grandma calls from the kitchen."

Finally, hand each group its bag and watch how your students unscramble the sentence puzzle and literally line the words up to form a sentence. Students may wish to compare their sentence with the original in the book. As a final activity, each group holds up each word and punctuation card to re-form its sentence so all groups can read the sentences aloud.

Another variation of sentence line-up is to give students different sections from sentence strips you've created and have them reconnect the sections to create a complete sentence.

For example: When it rains at night,/I/carefully count/the raindrops. After a rainstorm/I/play/in the mud puddles. As it rains,/raindrops/ smash/against the windowpane.

Students may rearrange the sentences as they originally appeared

or they may create other sentences, such as the following:

When it rains at night,/I/play/in the mud puddles. When it rains at night,/raindrops/smash/against the windowpane. As it rains,/I/play/in the mud puddles.

TREASURE HUNT

This activity will truly bring out the "treasure" in each of your students as they listen to one another's suggestions, plan and organize their hunt, and, finally, write their clues. (Picture clues work well, too, if some groups aren't ready to write all the words in their clues. Use the words *Go to* plus a picture.) For example, after reading *Alexander and the Wind-Up Mouse*, students can create a treasure hunt for the magical hidden purple pebble (a purple marble works nicely).

Students should be divided into groups to allow them to create hunts for each other. Remind them that the object of the hunt is not to stump the other groups but to provide clues that are clever yet clearly understandable.

Let each group take turns hiding its clues around the room while everyone else waits in the hallway. When the magic purple pebble has been found, students may want to take turns holding the pebble and making wishes.

HAPPY WORD DAY

You may want to expand the focus of a book by concentrating on one concept. If it seems illogical to expand your students' learning by narrowing its focus, let me provide you with the following example: After reading *The Village of Round and Square Houses*, students do extensive research and reading about houses. As a bonus, your students will learn about different customs and cultures, as well as the geography and languages of different countries. You can even include animal houses or make up some houses yourself, following the format used in *A House Is a House for Me*:

A picture frame is a house for a picture.
A stapler is a house for staples.

At the end of the day, each student shares what he or she has learned with the rest of the group, and all materials are gathered for display.

SCROUNGER

Student "scrounging" is well documented in several whole language books. Students scrounge when they copy words or letters from the environmental print in the classroom (labels, alphabet cards, books, posters, dictionaries, etc.) in order to create their own messages. Rather than think of scrounging as cheating, teachers need to encourage students to scrounge as their own needs dictate.

To make students more aware of the environmental print around the room and to encourage students to use it for their own learning, you might want to play scrounger. The rules are simple: Students create a message in which all words have been scrounged. The source of the words (or letters, if students are at that point) can be identified as well. Students may draw a picture of their source, copy the source's title, or use the source's label. After the message is created and sources documented, students pair up and "walk" each other through the message and sources. You may hear statements like "I got the word *where* from our Wall of Words chart, the word *is* from my learning log," and so forth.

Comprehension Strategy

A whole language instructional approach demands that teachers and students not expect the meaning of each word not to be hidden deeply within it as it stands mightily on the page; instead, students, and not the strokes of some typewriter or laser printer, give meaning to words. With this approach in place, then, how can teachers help students better comprehend and thereby create meaning? One way is through direct instruction that enables students to "think publicly" about language learning. Some of these direct-instruction activities are described below.

SWBS (PLOT CHART)

SWBS or Plot Chart is a comprehension technique developed by Dr. Barbara Schmidt of California State University at Sacramento. As she

describes in the monograph "Responses to Literature Grades K-8" (International Reading Association, 1989), the letters SWBS stand for SOMEBODY, WANTED, BUT, SO. Its use is especially suited to fictional materials such as short stories and plays. In fiction, there is a character (usually a person, animal, or thing) that represents the *s*: SOMEBODY. The SOMEBODY WANTED something, BUT there is a problem. The problem gets in the way of the SOMEBODY's getting what he or she WANTED, SO the SOMEBODY has to solve the problem. Often a chart is created like the one below, for *Madeline's Rescue*:

S (SOMEBODY):   Madeline, Miss Clavel, and the other eleven girls

W (WANTED):   to keep Genevieve, the dog that rescued Madeline

B (BUT):   the trustees make Genevieve leave the house

S (SO):   Madeline, Miss Clavel, and the other eleven girls search for Genevieve, who returns on her own and later has puppies—one for each little girl

An SWBS chart can be created after reading a story. Or students can create one before writing an original story or while preparing for storytelling.

BIG BOOKS

Commercially made Big Books are enlarged versions of children's books. The illustrations and type size are large enough for children to see and enjoy during shared reading time. Many popular children's books (the Caldecotts included) are now available in Big Book versions, and teachers have found them to be wonderful additions to their classroom libraries. A teacher's guide that offers suggestions for their use comes with most Big Books. Still, if you aren't familiar with how to use Big Books and want a little more background, you may wish to read Dr. Priscilla Lynch's book *Using Big Books and Predictable Books*.

In the past, Big Books were used almost exclusively with beginning readers, and their use with this population will certainly continue to grow. However, teachers of upper-elementary-grade students can gen-

erate some wonderful learning opportunities if they too use Big Books creatively in their classrooms. For example, I know a fifth-grade teacher who uses a Big Book of *Rosie's Walk* to teach prepositional phrases. When it comes to Big Books, the key is to make them part of your teaching style so you and your students get the most out of each one.

In addition to using commercially made Big Books, many teachers and their students create their own. The teacher prints the text on strips as students guide her, using the original book. Students choose which illustrations to do and then match the illustrations with the appropriate text. After the text is sequenced and the illustrations are coordinated, the pages are hung along the wall at the children's eye level. After a few days on display, the pages are taken down and sewn or stapled together with a title page and cover. Computer software that prints Big Book-size type is now available as well.

The same creation process can be used when creating Big Books from the children's original stories. In this way, your classroom library of Big Books will grow. For example, after reading *In the Forest*, teacher and students can create a Big Book entitled *In the Park*, and instead of the repetition of "When I went for a walk in the forest," students use "When I went for a walk in the park." (Maybe your park could have unicorns!) After the Big Book is created, you may want to perform a choral reading of *In the Park* with background parade music.

READING ALOUD TO CHILDREN

Reading a book aloud to your students may seem a rather simplistic thing to do to improve comprehension, but its merits shouldn't be overlooked. After all, it's natural to capitalize on the lap-time children grew up with when their parents read to them. Because reading aloud "brings the literature alive," it helps students understand characters and story action. It also helps them learn to listen with concentration. And many children's books are a lot like plays, in that both are incomplete until they've been performed live.

VENN DIAGRAM

The Venn diagram, used so well in other subject areas, is also an

appropriate device to use in language learning, to help students comprehend the concepts of comparing and contrasting. Similarities are
recorded in the intersecting portion of the circles while differences are
recorded in the two larger sections of each circle. For example, to compare
and contrast Alexander and Willy, the two mice in *Alexander and the
Wind-Up Mouse*:

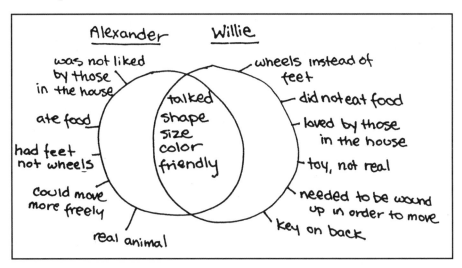

SPIKE IT

The purpose of Spike It is to use students' oral vocabulary to improve
their reading and writing vocabulary. In Spike It, the teacher takes a
word or phrase and puts the word *is* or *are* with it in the middle of a circle.
Students then brainstorm words to complete the sentence. These words
are written next to the spikes radiating from the circle. For example,
before reading *The Little House*, write "A house is" in the center of a circle:
(see diagram on the next page.)

Writing the students' ideas around the circle at the end of the spikes
is like a visual explosion of words from one simple idea. However, with
the Spike It method, teachers must probe for rich vocabulary words, as
the example demonstrates. Often many of the words your students
generate will be the very same words found in the storybook. In some
instances, too, your students will generate words used primarily during

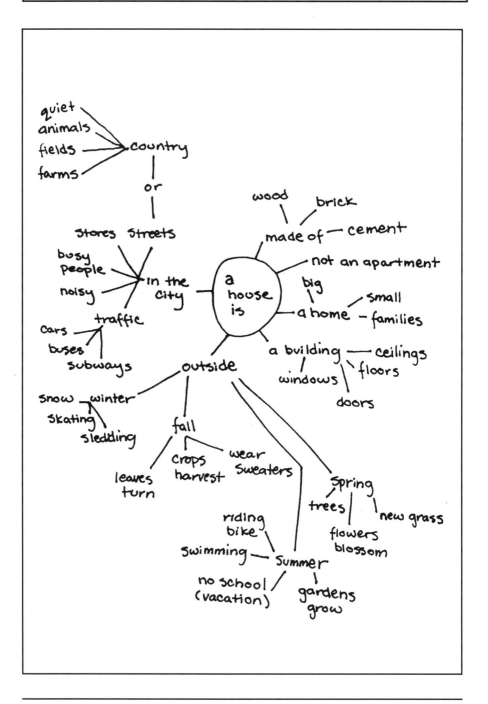

language-extension activities. Just think of the happy surprise in store for your students when they begin reading and writing—many of the words they "know" from their oral vocabulary begin to become a part of their reading and writing vocabularies!

This initial linking of oral vocabulary to reading and writing vocabularies becomes the basis for creating the Wall of Words. Some words for display from the above activity might include *families, apartment, building, windows, doors, street, small, big, wood, brick, spring, summer, winter, fall, grass, flowers, trees, garden, leaves, country, fields, streets, stores, cards, animals, quiet,* and *school.*

STORYTELLING

Storytelling is one of the most enjoyable ways for students to "write" stories. No need to worry about penmanship or spelling; no need for messy erasing.

Storytelling works well with large groups, small groups, pairs, or individuals. And even if every student bases his or her story on the same book, no two stories will be exactly alike.

Group storytelling helps students learn to sequence events, use complete sentences, and listen carefully.

For example, you may wish to do the following activity before reading *Free Fall*, a Caldecott book with no text:

The teacher begins the story, saying, "Last night I dreamed that I..." A student finishes the sentence and begins another. (The teacher may have to keep the story progressing with more setups until students get the hang of it.) Use connecting words like *then* and *next* to keep the story twisting and turning to a final conclusion. (Make sure everyone gets a chance to add a sentence.) Try tape recording the group's story. As they listen to the playback, stop the tape and have students edit the story while you write it on chart paper. The final draft can even be made into a Big Book.

Another way of encouraging group storytelling is to show the pictures of other nontext books, such as *The Gray Lady and the Strawberry Snatcher* or *Truck,* and have students create text to accompany the illustrations. Smaller groups can create different stories to accompany

the same illustrations, providing an opportunity to compare and contrast to check students' thinking.

Or you could have students retell a story they've read. However, before students tell stories themselves, you may wish to have a storyteller as a guest speaker or demonstrate storytelling yourself. In any case, stories such as *Mirandy and Brother Wind, The Bremen-Town Musicians,* and *The Amazing Bone,* as well as many of the fairy tales and folktales in the Caldecott collection, are suitable for storytelling.

Story-Structure Strategy

The purpose of the story-structure strategy is to give students one more way to figure out how language works.

As a result of language experiences, students come to expect print to start at the top of the page and move from left to right. by introducing students to story structures, they will also come to expect stories to have structures and to know that these structures, once learned, can be applied to many stories regardless of setting, author, illustrations, or characters.

Please note that the use of the term "story structure" isn't to be confused with the term "text structure." A great deal of research has been conducted regarding the teaching of expository text structure. (An excellent article is "Teaching Text Structure to Improve Reading and Writing," by Armbruster, Anderson and Ostertag, *The Reading Teacher,* November 1989.) Consequently, "story structure" is merely a tool to get students to think critically even though it employs some of the same terms used in text structure research. In addition, "story structure" finds some of its roots in basic literature patterns such as "rhyme/rhythm," "time sequence," and "repetitive." (A nice list can be found in Jane Baskwill and Paulette Whitman's book *A Guide to Classroom Publishing* [Scholastic]).

Activities designed to help students recognize specific structures and the thinking strategies associated with them are detailed in Chapters 5 to 11.

SEQUENCE OF EVENTS

Most books have a structure based on a sequence of events. The story's events occur first, second, third, and so forth until the concluding event. Books that have a sequence of events as their dominant structure include *Where the Wild Things Are, A Story A Story, The Polar Express,* and *The Snowy Day.*

LIST AND SEQUENCE

Books that list items, ideas, or characters and then sequence them use a list-and-sequence structure. Some Caldecotts with this dominant structure are *On Market Street, One Fine Day, The House That Jack Built,* and *Ox-Cart Man.*

COMPARING-CONTRASTING

Comparing-contrasting is best done when students compare and contrast characters within books or even compare and contrast different versions of the same story. However, comparing-contrasting is included here as a separate category because of Robert McCloskey's wonderful book *Blueberries for Sal,* in which McCloskey bases his story on different characters involved in parallel actions.

Although not based on the comparing-contrasting structure, Arnold Lobel's story "The Lost Button" in *Frog and Toad Are Friends* provides an excellent opportunity for students to compare and contrast different buttons. (See Chapter 8 for details.)

Don't forget to compare and contrast the art in different books, as well as the setting and tone. For example, *Owl Moon* is very different from *Ben's Trumpet,* yet both stories are about young boys; *Many Moons* and *King Bidgood's in the Bathtub* are equally different, yet each has a king as its main character.

QUESTION-ANSWER

The question-answer structure is rather easy to identify. The author poses a question and then devotes the remainder of the book to looking for an answer. Two wonderful examples are *Have You Seen My Duckling?* and *King Bidgood's in the Bathtub.*

RHYME AND REPETITION

Books with rhymes that repeat themselves are also easy to identify and a lot of fun to read and listen to. Real favorites are *Drummer Hoff* and *May I Bring a Friend?*

GENERAL STATEMENT AND ELABORATION

Freight Train, by Donald Gates, is a good example of this story structure. Gates makes a brief statement about the freight train and then uses a few rhythmic words to elaborate.

This category, like comparing-contrasting, is limited in its examples. However, using a general statement and elaboration structure is one way to help students create their own original story picture books. The technique is described in Chapter 7.

PROBLEM SOLUTION

Leo Lionni's *Swimmy* is a wonderful example of the problem-solution structure, not only because it shows little fish joining together to solve their problem—being eaten alive—but also because it demonstrates how thinking is used to solve problems. Other good books with problem-solution structures include *It Could Always Be Worse* and *Lon Po Po*.

CAUSE-EFFECT

The cause-effect structure is often used in conjunction with the problem-solution structure. In Tomie dePaola's *Strega Nona*, Big Anthony's inability to pay attention caused him to miss seeing Strega Nona perform the entire magic pasta-pot spell. The result (effect)? A near-disaster when the pasta pot boiled out of control. The solution to this problem? Big Anthony ate the pasta away!

Listening-Lab Strategies

Students listen all day long, to teachers and to one another. They also "listen" with an inner voice as they create meaning while reading. Engaging that inner voice while still physically listening is the benefit students get when they listen to tapes and records as they follow along

with a book. You can use tapes and books that the students have made themselves, that you have made, or that you have purchased. The important thing is to have a variety of them from which students can choose.

Another way of combining books and listening is to create "book orchestrations." Choose a piece of music that conveys the tone and atmosphere of a book and use it as background while you read the book aloud. Or you might want to record sound effects on tape and play them at appropriate moments as you read. If your school library media center or area education agency doesn't have what you need, check with your local library. Many have records and tapes, including sound-effects records.

Finally, try to include lots of records and tapes of songs and poems, along with their word sheets, in your listening library. You'll find these to be some of your students' best-loved and most-used language resources.

Performing-Arts Strategy

Given a safe, praise-filled environment, almost all students will respond to the call to perform in choral reading, Readers' Theater, or a simple play. So grab your video camera and clear away the desks!

CHORAL READING

In choral reading the text of a book is divided among groups of students who chime in at different parts during the presentation. Besides using individual copies, the text can be printed on chart paper and color-coded, or it can be printed on an overhead. A student "conductor" cues each group and moves the reading along just like a symphony conductor. Some appropriate books for choral reading are *If All the Seas Were One Sea, Drummer Hoff, Why Mosquitoes Buzz in People's Ears,* and *The House That Jack Built.*

READERS' THEATER

Readers' Theater differs from choral reading in that parts are

assigned to different characters. Text may be assigned to groups, as well, to add variety to the performance.

One book for Readers' Theater that also affords an excellent opportunity to discuss sexual stereotyping is *What Do You Say, Dear? A Book of Manners for All Occasions* by Sesyle Joslin. You can counteract the book's stereotypes by first discussing sexual stereotyping and then having boys and girls take turns being the narrator. Then half the class can ask, "What do you say, dear?" while the other half gives the appropriate response. Who knows? Maybe your students will learn a little something about good manners too!

You can also use posters, signs, placards, and other visuals when creating your Readers' Theater presentations. In addition, character diaries and letters your students have created can be used as scripts.

PLAYS

Almost any book can be acted out if students are allowed to use their fertile imaginations—and the teacher can find the floor space! Don't worry about costumes and props; let the students concentrate on character development. To this end, encourage students to "get into character" by challenging them to speak and move just like the character would if he or she came to life.

Because they require several student actors, some good choices for plays include *Stone Soup, Frog Went A-Courtin', Sylvester and the Magic Pebble, Strega Nona, Swimmy*, and *Frederick*.

PUPPETS AND PANTOMIME

Using puppets to have students recreate a story or create one improvisational style is a wonderful "natural" language activity. Once again, materials to create the puppets do not have to be elaborate and expensive. Construction paper, glue, and a brown paper bag do nicely and save the remainder of the time for the performance.

Pantomime is another way of using language of a different sort—body language. Hold up *Owl Moon* and ask your students to show you the tone of the book or how the book "feels." They may just bring their knees to their chins, curl their arms around their bodies, and smile warmly. On

the other hand, ask them to show you the feeling of *Where the Wild Things Are*, and you may see them literally jumping in the aisles!

Visual-Arts Strategy

Students have been coloring, cutting, pasting, and painting in classrooms for a long time. Not only do they use their motor skills, but they also use a lot of their thinking skills. In fact, much of the same thinking that students do when they write is used in the planning and organizing of a visual-arts project.

POSTERS AND SIGNS

Posters and signs are everywhere in our world, and they should be everywhere in your classroom and school. Posters and signs convey succinct messages with graphics and text, making them ideal literacy resources. Here are some examples:

◆ After reading *Houses from the Sea*, students read more about shells and create posters, describing and drawing different shells.

◆ After reading *Stone Soup*, students create posters that list ingredients and cooking directions for their own versions of stone soup.

◆ After reading *The Little House*, students create signs (road, traffic, store) they'd find in the city and signs they'd find in the country.

BOOK ILLUSTRATIONS

Nowhere will you find such a variety of art styles as in the Caldecott collection. Without looking at the name of the artist, it's often easy to recognize books illustrated by Tomie dePaola, Dr. Seuss, John Steptoe, and Trina Schart Hyman. Because many Caldecotts are illustrated by the same artist, you can compare the art of one story with the art of another, entirely different story. For example, ask students to compare the art in *One Fine Day* with that in *The Contest*. (Can your students see the same woman in both books?)

Another activity using Caldecott art is to have students practice

their predicting skills by covering a book's text and creating a story simply by "reading" the illustrations. For example, have students create a SWBS chart using the illustrations in Lynd Ward's *The Biggest Bear*. Next, read the story aloud and create another SWBS chart based on the actual text. Compare and contrast the two charts.

PROJECTS

Science projects and arts-and-crafts projects are hands-on learning experiences in which students demonstrate a wide variety of thinking skills. They hypothesize, build models, plan, organize, speculate, analyze, and apply principles. Try these examples:

◆ After they've read *Bear Party*, have students create party masks and then use the masks to act out the story.

◆ After they've read *The Storm Book*, have students read more about weather and conduct weather-related experiments.

OBJECTS

Using objects to enhance the reading of a story is similar to a speaker's lighting a candle during the introduction of a fire-safety speech. The object gets the students' attention and provides a smooth transition from reading to discussing. For example, imagine your students' delight if you drew a small silver bell from your pocket after you read Chris Van Allsburg's *The Polar Express* or if a high-school student popped into class and played the trumpet after you read *Ben's Trumpet* !

In Conclusion

The strategies and activities described in this chapter are not the only ones available to whole language teachers, although they do represent "prime-time teaching." They require flexibility, creativity, organization, and dedication—the very same qualities you possess as a flexible, creative, organized, and dedicated professional teacher!

A Three Stage Approach to Literacy:
Book Introduction, Structure Recognition, and Language Immersion

The literacy model in this chapter is of macro-design. In other words, it does not offer a daily schedule or suggest a method of organizing classroom resources. Instead, it describes how your instruction can be organized to allow you to be flexible and creative.

The three-stage model works for all Caldecotts and assumes the following: You and your students are reading other books and poems (together as well as independently); that books are checked out of the classroom library for nightly reading; that journal writing and learning logs are used regularly; that books are read and reread as requested by students; that teacher-student conferencing is taking place; and that evaluation is an ongoing process. Finally, the model assumes that your purpose is to focus instruction on reading, writing, speaking, listening, and thinking.

Stage I: Book Introduction

One of the main purposes of the book-introduction stage is to get students interested and excited about the book you are introducing. After all, if you're not excited about a book, your students will know. So make sure you choose books that you'll enjoy reading over and over again. Another important purpose is to "establish set."

ESTABLISHING SET

Establishing set occurs when old learning is recalled to help new learning take place. Establishing set is not a new idea and relates to psychologist Johann Friedrich Herbart's development of the concept of apperception. Herbart believed that the mind was organized and represented a composite effect of all past experiences, and that we come to know, understand, and interpret something new in terms of what we already know.

Consequently, Herbart developed a model of instruction, the first step of which Wilhelm Rein later called "Preparation" (explained in English by Harold B. Dunkel in *Herbart and Education*). In Preparation, teachers alert students to what they already know in reference to what is about to be learned.

One of today's leading learning psychologists, Robert Gagné, in

(continued)

Principles of Instructional Design, incorporates this same concept into the second step of his instructional model, which is entitled "Events of Instruction." During this step, called "Stimulating Recall of Prerequisite Learning," teachers ask questions to help students recall any prior knowledge and learning that will aid students in new learning. Having students recall prior knowledge as an aid in learning new knowledge is a vital step when introducing a new book to them.

In addition to getting students excited about the book and establishing set, the book-introduction stage is designed to accomplish two other goals. By asking questions that allow students to tell what they already know about the topic discussed in the book, you discover the students' "world knowledge" and get a firsthand, detailed list of the students' oral vocabulary, which in turn can be a starting point from which to assess the scope of language growth.

Step 1: Before showing students Ezra Jack Keats's *The Snowy Day*, say, "Today's book is about snow. Tell me about an experience you've had with snow." (If you live where snow is rare, ask your students to tell you what they think snow feels like. Also ask them to tell you about snow they've seen on TV or in books.)

Listen carefully to your students' vocabulary and join in their enthusiasm. Keep in mind that you may wish to prompt students' recall of many of their words for use in Step 2. Try to let everyone who wants to speak get a turn.

Step 2: Spike It. Print the words "Snow is" in a circle with several radiating spikes. Then ask, "When I say the words 'Snow is...,' what words can you think of to complete the sentence?"

Step 3: Record the words on chart paper or on an overhead. (These words need to be retrieved at a later time.) Continue to probe student responses to generate words that are used in the story and that students will use for the language-extension activities to come. For example, when a student says that snow is cold, you could respond by saying, "Yes, snow is cold. Can anyone name some special things you have to wear because snow is cold?" Continue to probe for rich vocabulary.

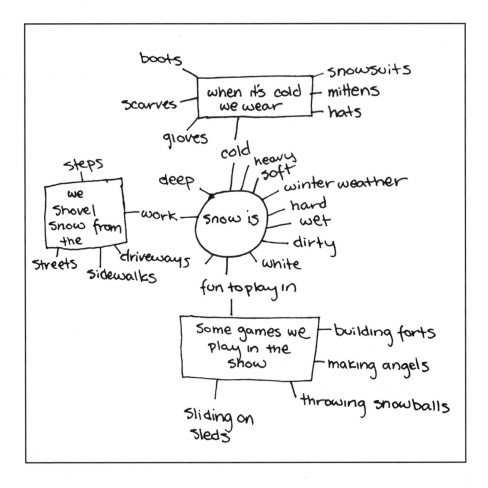

After the students generate the words for Spike It and you record them, praise them for doing a good job!

Step 4: Show students the book. State the title, author, and illustrator. Look at the title page and explain the publisher. After they've viewed the cover art and heard the book's title, ask students to make predictions about the book's plot and characters. Write their predictions on the board or chart paper with the students' initials next to them. (Students who are familiar with the book are asked to "keep it a surprise" for others.)

Step 5: Using all the dramatics you can muster, read the book aloud to the children. Bring the book alive with your voice, facial expressions, and gestures!

This first time through the book, it's a good idea not to stop for discussion. You are modeling for the students, and they need to hear the language rhythm without interruption. During this first shared reading experience, you may want to use a Big Book or the original book with an opaque projector so all can see and enjoy it. (Have multiple copies of the book available for individual as well as small-group reading times.)

Step 6: Ask students to react to the book. Get students to go beyond "I liked it." Ask what it was about the book they liked and why. Then return to the list of predictions and see which ones were accurate.

Step 7: The final step during the book-introduction stage is to read the book again as a group. Use your voice to cue predictable words. Have students join in on any repetitive parts and ask students to make guesses about words and what will happen next. You may also want to begin asking thinking questions to help students add meaning to the text. (With longer books such as *Jumanji* you may want to read only parts of the story as a group.)

By following the book-introduction stage of the model, you've gotten students excited about the book, helped them recall prior knowledge, generated a list of vocabulary words, read the book aloud to students, given students an opportunity to react to the book, and, finally, helped students read and think about the book. You've done a lot of things, but what you've really done is helped students see themselves as capable learners and, above all, gotten them excited about reading!

Stage II: Structure Recognition

As its name implies, during structure recognition students focus on the structure of letters and words as well as the structure of the story. Now is the time for deep processing with an eye toward structure of different kinds.

Step 1: The structure-recognition stage begins with another group reading of the book. During this reading, you may wish to use some oral cloze procedures by masking different words or passages. (An excellent description of masking and oral cloze can be found in Don Holdaway's *The Foundations of Literacy*.) Display the word lists generated during the Spike It activity and ask students to circle any of the words on the list that they find while reading the text. (This is a lot of fun. Students get SO excited when they make a match!)

Step 2: During this step, students go through all the words on the Spike It list and choose which ones to keep for display as their Wall of Words. (Don't be surprised if students do not want to discard many

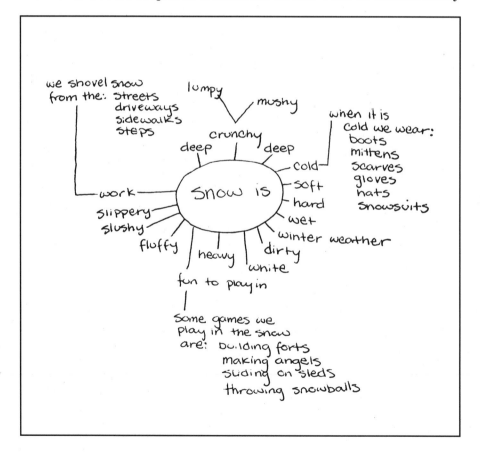

words. After all, these are "their words," and they don't like having them discarded.)

The teacher can then choose to recopy these words on different-colored blocks of paper or use different-colored ink in order to classify the words. A drawing of the front cover of the book along with its title can be displayed with the words.

Next, students copy the classified words in their learning logs. Some students may want to copy the entire list into their logs while others may want to record just a few. (You may yourself have a few specific words that you want every student to record.) Students are then given pieces of oaktag on which they may write any words they claim as their own. The words are put into their word bags. (These are the same word bags used in adopt-a-word.) Older students might want to keep specially decorated "word book" notebooks along with their learning logs instead of word bags.

Step 3: This step focuses on each book's story structure and the strategies you can use to teach those structures. The main purpose in teaching story structures is to help students think about the structures and generalize them to other stories.

In other words, a student reads three books with problem-solution structures, such as *Stone Soup, Swimmy*, and *Bear Party*, during shared book time and is taught to recognize the problem-solution structure. Then he or she can apply that structure to *Anatole and the Cat* and begin asking questions such as "How will Anatole solve his problem?" Getting students to think on their own while they're reading is the goal of teaching story structures.

Teaching Structure

To teach structure, first determine the type of story structure a book has and then select the appropriate thinking strategy to teach the structure. Structures and thinking taught in this way enable students not only to learn the structure of any given book but also to learn a critical-thinking skill. In general, you may want to use the following combinations:

(Continued)

Structure	Thinking Strategy
List and sequence	Listing, classifying, sequencing, categorizing
Sequence of events	Sequencing, explaining cause and effect
Problem-solution	Problem solution, cause and effect
Comparing-contrasting	Comparing and contrasting
Cause-effect	Explaining cause and effect, problem solution
Question-answer	Problem solution, sequencing
Rhyme and repetition	Listing, classifying, sequencing, categorizing
General statement and elaboration	Comparing and contrasting, listing

This is a generic list. You must treat each book individually and use whatever strategy works best for your students and for the chosen book. In addition, thinking skills are discussed in Chapter 4, and the various thinking strategies used to teach structure are demonstrated in Chapters 5 to 11.

Step 4: Students reread the book as a group. (Individual copies of the book are recommended.) Each page is devoured, and special attention is paid to grammar, spelling, punctuation, phrasing, vocabulary, word usage, and letter-sound associations. Although you and your students have done all these things at other times while reading the book together, during this step you may want to bring all these elements together to reinforce them in the context of the whole book.

Now also is the time to work with phonics if you wish. For example, in Keats's *The Snowy Day* you may wish to teach students the two sounds for *ow,* as represented by *snow* and *down,* two words found in the story. You may also wish to teach the two-letter consonants of *sn* and *sm* as represented by the words *snow, smacking,* and *smiling.* Finally, since the word *angel* plays an important role in the story, now may be a good time to introduce students to the *j* sound for *g.* These phonics lessons in meaningful context are more natural than isolated drill sheets.

Step 5: In the final step in structure recognition, students retell the

story as a group. The teacher begins by holding up the closed book so everyone can see the cover and says, "Listen carefully as I tell you the story of *The Snowy Day*. One winter morning Peter woke up and..." The teacher stops and gives the book to a student, who then adds to the story. After the student tells a small portion of the story, she too stops and hands the book to another student. This process continues until the complete story is told. An alternative is to create an oral story that is a variation of the original.

Regardless of the story you choose to tell, however, this step is designed to encourage students to listen carefully and think sequentially, as well as to give students an opportunity to speak in a group setting.

Stage III: Language Immersion

Your students immerse themselves in language during various language-extension activities. Consequently, whether students are writing a shopping list, reading recipes, or creating posters, the purpose of a language-extension activity is to integrate the language processes so students come to "own" words.

At the same time, students do not learn language simply because a teacher tells it to them; they learn language to meet their literacy needs at hand. So while students are busy "owning" words, the teacher is busily shaping the environment and creating literacy opportunities by providing students with additional books and poems, allowing students time to listen to recorded books and songs, encouraging student conferencing, and continuing to conference with students herself. In addition, during language immersion you have the opportunity to provide direct instruction. For example, when the need arises, teach students how to use reference materials, or show them the steps to follow when planning a project. If a small group of students continue to have difficulty punctuating dialogue, gather them together for specific instruction in this area.

Because a number of different language-immersion activities were mentioned in Chapter 2, a list will not be provided here. Instead, several activities using authentic literacy resources are described in detail later in this book. You may wish to use some of them as they are written,

modify them, or design your own—whatever meets your students' literacy needs. It's important to note that some teachers may think the activities described are too difficult, while others may think they are too easy. At the same time, some teachers will use one book at the first-grade level while others will use the same book at the second-grade level. All of that is fine, because with whole language instruction, literacy isn't a race!

REINFORCEMENT

Reinforcement is the final step in the model. It is included as part of the language-immersion stage because, in the most practical sense, it's language learning that's gone home for nurturing. More than just homework, reinforcement is an attempt to apply to the real world literacy learning that has taken place in the classroom.

In order to accomplish this, parents must have a clear understanding of what literacy is all about and how what you're doing in the classroom helps their children become literate individuals. (A meeting at the beginning of the school year and frequent home contacts help establish and keep open the lines of communication.)

When you ask parents to reinforce their child's literacy learning, they need to know what to do, how to do it, and why doing an activity that encourages literate behavior will help their child. A note explaining to parents how they can build upon what has been happening in the classroom can often be a useful way to involve parents in their child's education. (It's true you probably won't get 100 percent home involvement at the beginning or ever, but even if you get 15 percent, it's a start.)

For example, send a brief letter home stating the following: "In class this week, we have been reading *The Snowy Day*, by Ezra Jack Keats. We have also been reading and writing the names of different pieces of clothing children wear when they go out to play in the snow. To help your child read and write the names of other pieces of clothing, go through your child's closet and drawers with him or her and have him or her write the names of different pieces of clothing. First, let your child write the name of the piece of clothing using invented spelling, and then ask your child if he or she would like to see the words using "grown-up" spelling. Write

the word using conventional spelling below your child's word. (Don't erase your child's word!)

FINAL COMMENTS

Like all people who design good instructional models, I encourage you to modify any part of the model to fit your teaching style and your students' needs. For example, a book such as *Jumanji* may not need to be read as a group more than once or twice, because it is for more experienced readers. Just remember, the model is like a suit of clothes— if it doesn't fit, make adjustments!

Whole Language and Thinking: The Critical Connection

In *Teaching Thinking Across the Curriculum*, Vincent Ruggiero defines thinking as "any mental activity that helps formulate or solve a problem, make a decision, or fulfill a desire to understand; it is a searching for answers, a reaching for meaning." In light of this definition, we teachers need to ask ourselves how much of our teaching really helps students search for answers and reach for meaning. In addition, we need to ask how often we solve our students' problems and make decisions for them in our efforts to "cover the material."

Believe me, I am guilty of "expediency teaching." In my first year, I gave a paper-and-pencil test on listening skills! However, other educators are discovering that incorporating thinking into their lessons doesn't prevent them from covering the material but, in fact, helps students learn the material more effectively.

Four Ways Teachers Can Promote Thinking

Research suggests several ways teachers can promote student thinking. Four suggestions are that teachers do the following:

◆ Design and use materials, activities, and modes of instruction that require students to think.
◆ Ask questions that require students to think beyond recalling information.
◆ Extend the wait time after asking a question and before responding to a student's answer.
◆ Model thinking for students.

As you can see, none of the areas mentioned above requires teachers to delete part of the curriculum or turn their classrooms upside down. Instead, they have more to do with changing teachers' behavior than with anything else in the classroom.

MATERIALS AND MODES

Teachers can promote thinking by designing and using teaching materials that require students to think—not just to think in order to apply discrete skills but to think for various reasons and in a variety of ways.

55

So instead of presenting students with a worksheet on which they must capitalize the names of streets, teachers can give students city maps with which students can plan a route from their home street to another destination, such as the school. Students can then write out their set of instructions, which should include properly capitalized street names (and other proper nouns, if appropriate). For example: "To get to Main School from my house, go west on Washington Street and pass the Valley Shopping Mall. Next, turn south onto Monroe Street and then west onto Main Street." With this activity, students apply some basic capitalization rules required in the language-arts curriculum and also develop some map-reading skills. At the same time, they are required to read, write, and think.

In addition to using "thought-full" materials, teachers can promote thinking by using different modes of instruction. In other words, teachers can arrange opportunities for students to learn individually, in small groups, and in large groups. "Orchestrating learning" becomes the job of the teacher. For example, students can read a story as a group, break into small groups for language-extension activities, and then respond individually to the literature by writing in their journals.

ASKING QUESTIONS

Another way in which teachers can help improve student thinking is by asking a variety of questions that require students to engage in various cognitive behaviors.

Falkof and Moss ("When Teachers Tackle Thinking Skills," *Educational Leadership*, 1984) reported that 80 to 85 percent of all questions asked by teachers were on a factual level. In other words, all but 15 to 20 percent of teachers' questions were at the knowledge level of Bloom's taxonomy (*Taxonomy of Educational Objectives, Handbook I: Cognitive Domain*, by Benjamin S. Bloom et al.), which represents the lowest level of learning outcomes in the cognitive domain. While asking factual questions is quite necessary, concentrating only on factual questions robs students of opportunities to think critically and to create original ideas. *So what's the alternative?*

Arthur L. Costa presents an alternative in the wonderful, must-read book *Developing Minds: A Resource Book for Teaching Thinking.* Teachers can use Costa's three-phase "Model of Intellectual Functioning" to help develop and monitor the different types of questions they ask in their classrooms. His model distinguishes questions appropriate for use during the "Data Input Phase," the "Processing Phase," and the "Output Phase" of thinking.

Costa's model and Bloom's taxonomy can be viewed together in the box on this page. As close examination reveals, using Costa's three-phase model to develop and monitor your classroom questions won't deviate from what you already know as a teacher. What it will do is help you condition yourself to ask questions that go beyond the input phase or knowledge stage of thinking.

Costa

Data Input Phase   Processing Phase   Output Phase

Bloom

Knowledge   Comprehension   Application

Analysis   Evaluation

Synthesis

(From *Toward a Model of Human Intellectual Functioning*)

Below are examples of some of the most useful questions and statements that can be developed based in part on Costa's model. A more thorough explanation of his model as well as additional examples of questions and statements can be found in his *Developing Minds: A Resource Book for Teaching Thinking.*

INPUT: During the input phase, students gather and recall information. Teachers writing behavioral objectives based on Bloom's taxonomy use some of the following terms: defining, describing, listing, identifying, naming, matching, selecting, and completing.

Question/Statement	Cognitive Behavior
Name the main characters in Robert McCloskey's *Blueberries for Sal.*	Naming
Describe the stallion who was the leader of the wild horses in Paul Goble's *The Girl Who Loved Wild Horses.*	Describing

Match the following author-illustrators and their books:
    The Polar Express
    The Amazing Bone
    Strega Nona
	Matching
	
	William Steig
	Tomie dePaola
	Chris Van Allsburg

Count the number of animals you can find in Suse MacDonald's *Alphabetics.*	Counting
List all the items the young shoppers bought in Arnold Lobel's *On Market Street.*	Listing
Define the word *brave* as it is used in Jane Yolen's book *Owl Moon.*	Defining
Which words on this page from Marie Hall Ets's book *In the Forest* have *-ing* at the end?	Selecting
The book *Mufaro's Beautiful Daughters* was written and illustrated by _____.	Completing
Using the book cover from *Frog and Toad Are Friends*, identify which character is Frog and which	Identifying

character is Toad.

Recite the recurring line in Julian Scheer's book *Rain Makes Applesauce.*	Reciting

PROCESSING: During the processing phase students use the information they have gathered to analyze, synthesize, compare and contrast, and draw conclusions based on cause and effect. In addition, students summarize and classify information. Teachers writing behavioral objectives based on Bloom's taxonomy use some of the following terms: comparing, contrasting, inferring, classifying, explaining, sequencing, and summarizing.

Question/Statement	Cognitive Behavior
Compare these two Red Riding Hood stories: Trina Schart Hyman's *Little Red Riding Hood and* Ed Young's *Lon Po Po: A Red-Riding Hood Story from China.*	Comparing
Contrast these two Rumpelstiltskin stories: Paul O. Zelinsky's *Rumpelstiltskin* and Harve Zemach's*Duffy and the Devil.*	Contrasting
Explain why Frederick did not help the other mice gather corn, nuts, wheat, and straw in Leo Lionni's book *Frederick.*	Explaining
What personal characteristic of Big Anthony's causes him to miss seeing all of Strega Nona's magic spell in Tomie dePaola's book *Strega Nona?*	Explaining cause

What effect did performing for his grandchildren in the attic have on the grandfather in Karen Ackerman's book *Song and Dance Man?*

Explaining effect

What can you infer in Cynthia Rylant's book *The Relatives Came* as to how the families feel about each other?

Inferring

Sequence from beginning to end the following eight events from Gail E. Haley's book *A Story A Story.*

Sequencing

- Ananse delivers Oseobo, Mmboro, and Mnoatla to the Sky God.
- Ananse captures Mmboro, the hornets-who-sting-like-fire.
- Ananse scatters the stories to the corners of the world.
- Ananse spins a web to the sky to ask the Sky God for his stories.
- Ananse carves and prepares the wooden doll.
- The Sky God declares all the stories to be Spider Stories.
- Ananse captures Mnoatla the Fairy-whom-no-man-sees.
- Ananse captures Oseobo, the leopard-of-the-terrible-teeth.

Classify the following books into two different groups:
    Umbrella
    The Biggest Bear
    Where the Wild Things Are
    Madeline's Rescue

Classifying

Owl Moon
The Snowy Day
A Chair for My Mother
Mr. Rabbit and the Lovely Present

Categorize the books listed above into two categories: 　　Books with a female lead character 　　Books with a male lead character	Categorizing
What other kinds of activities besides games such as the one described in Chris Van Allsburg's book *Jumanji* require that we follow rules?	Making analogies
How can you organize information on a poster describing the different shells in Alice E. Goudey's book *Houses from the Sea* so others can read the poster easily?	Organizing
What characteristics do you see in Molly Bang's illustrations in *The Gray Lady and the Strawberry Snatcher* that lead you to believe that she also illustrated *Ten, Nine, Eight*?	Distinguishing
Summarize Dianne Snyder's message in her book *The Boy of the Three-Year Nap*.	Summarizing

OUTPUT: During the output phase students use their imaginations and make judgments while applying information in new situations. Teachers writing behavioral objectives based on Bloom's taxonomy use some of the following terms: imagining, planning, evaluating, predicting, and inventing.

Question/Statement	Cognitive Behavior
In Ilse Plume's book *The Bremen-Town Musicians,* the animals went to sleep "each according to his own idea of comfort." Give examples of other animals sleeping each "according to his own idea of comfort."	Applying a principle
Invent different kinds of fish for Dr. Seuss's book *McElligot's Pool.*	Inventing
What do you think would happen if we took the illustrations from Maurice Sendak's book *Where the Wild Things Are* and put them with the words from Ezra Jack Keats's book *The Snowy Day?*	Hypothesizing
Janice May Udry describes how wonderful trees are in her book *A Tree Is Nice.* Imagine what life would be like if we destroyed all the trees.	Imagining
Which of these two covers do you think is more humorous: Joseph Low's cover for *Mice Twice* or James Marshall's cover for *Goldilocks and the Three Bears?* Explain why you think this.	Judging illustrations
What can we say about all the stories in Arnold Lobel's book *Frog and Toad Are Friends?*	Generalizing
In Marcia Brown's book *Once A Mouse...* was the hermit's	Evaluating

decision to turn the tiger back
into a mouse a fair decision?
Why or why not?

After reading Chris Van Allsburg's   Speculating
book *Jumanji*, tell what you think
will happen to Daniel and Walter
Budwing in light of what Mrs.
Budwing said about them.

At the end of Donald Hall's book   Predicting
Ox-Cart Man, it is May and the
family is planting potatoes and the
geese are dropping their feathers.
Predict what the farmer will do four
months later, when it is October.

After reading Marcia Brown's book   Planning
Stone Soup, plan and execute a meal
with stone soup as the main course.

As this list attests, teachers can use a variety of questions and statements to promote student thinking. And although becoming skilled at asking a variety of questions takes time, teachers report that the time is well spent because students become more involved in their own learning.

EXTENDING WAIT TIME

A third way teachers can help improve student thinking is to extend the wait time after asking a question and before responding to a student's answer. This suggestion may seem almost too easy. However, Costa and Lowery state in *Techniques for Teaching Thinking* that "many teachers wait only one or two seconds after having asked a question before they either call on another student, ask another question, or give the answer to the question themselves." And upon receiving a response, teachers wait less than one full second before commenting. It seems, then, that we teachers are somewhat uncomfortable with silent thinking time and are

almost conditioned to "fill the air with learning."

Consider the above research in light of what Costa reports from Rowe's study "Wait Times and Rewards as Instructional Variables: Their Influence on Language, Logic and Fate Control" *(Journal of Research in Science Teaching*, 1974): When teachers wait for longer periods of time after asking a question or receiving a response, "students tend to respond with whole sentences and complete thoughts." In addition, "student-to-student interaction is greater, the number of questions students ask increases, and shy students begin to contribute."

With these kinds of student responses reported as a result of extending the wait time, it would seem to be in the best interest of student thinking for teachers to wait. Just wait three to ten seconds and then listen for the learning!

TEACHERS MODELING THINKING

Teaching-by-example is extremely powerful teaching. If a teacher models the problem-solving steps of stating the problem, considering solutions, choosing a solution, and implementing the solution, students witness firsthand how to solve problems. In addition, if that same teacher exposes his thinking by actually thinking out loud while solving the problem, students also benefit from the teacher's oral explanation of his metacognitive processes.

With all this thinking going on, it may be time to evaluate the kind of thinking you model for your students. After all, if we teachers improve our thinking and our modeling, will our students be far behind?

One Final Note

Encouraging student thinking is a natural part of whole language instruction. Certainly, the suggestions made in this chapter will take some effort as you begin to develop a variety of questions and modify your behavior to enhance student thinking. But realizing that you as a classroom teacher have the incredible power to get students to really think should encourage you and move you onward as you create and nurture your thinking classroom!

BEFORE YOU CONTINUE...

Having read Chapters 1 through 4, you may be eager to jump ahead and read only the chapters containing the Caldecott books you plan to use in your classroom. However, I urge you to take just a few minutes to read Chapter 5 completely before moving on to the remaining chapters. Chapter 5 will take you step-by-step, detail-by-detail through the model, using *On Market Street,* a book for beginning readers, and *Strega Nona,* a book for more experienced readers. The chapter is designed to get you more comfortable with the model and its application to different books. The 15 Caldecott books used to demonstrate the instructional model described in Chapter 3 were chosen for a number of reasons.

First, they represent the wide variety of topics, tones, and styles found within the Caldecott collection of books. In addition, the 15 books contain art ranging from bold to beautiful as well as a variety of main characters ranging from children to animals, with a truck and a train thrown in for good measure!

Moreover, the 15 books appeal to children in grades K-4 and lend themselves to language extension activities that not only utilize a wide variety of literacy materials but also promote the integration of reading writing, listening, speaking, and thinking.

Some of the instructional areas and activities of focus include the following:

K-1
On Market Street
   -reinforcing beginning sounds
   -planning, organizing, and creating lists and posters
Truck
   -interpreting environmental print
   -planning and creating environmental print
Freight Train
   -creating elaborated sentences
   -completing rhyming sentences

1-3

Ox-Cart Man
  -utilizing forms and charts
  -imagining living in an earlier time
A Chair for My Mother
  -explaining problem-solution
  -planning, organizing, and creating menus and display ads
Crow Boy
  -sequencing events to create an autobiography
  -utilizing nonfiction resource materials for research
Blueberries for Sal
  -explaining comparing and contrasting
  -using cloze procedure
Frog and Toad Together
  -explaining cause-effect using the Venn diagram
  -creating a SWBS chart to organize original story writing
The Snowy Day
  -speaking in front of a group
  -writing a sequel story
Make Way for Ducklings
  -utilizing maps to describe geographic directions
  -implementing a four-part planning process
Where the Wild Things Are
  -planning, organizing, and creating a brochure
  -conducting a choral reading

3-4

Jumanji
  -explaining problem solution
  -evaluating and writing game instructions and newspaper stories
Lon Po Po: A Red-Riding Hood Story from China
  -comparing and contrasting Red-Riding Hood stories
  -planning, organizing, and creating Chinese language charts
Strega Nona
  -using synectics to write pasta poems
  -imagining a "magical" invention

On Market Street

Strega Nona

On Market Street

Anita and Arnold Lobel's book *On Market Street* will give your students a literacy-shopping experience they won't soon forget! Using the alphabetical listing of the intricate, whimsically illustrated items, students reinforce beginning consonant sounds, learn how to punctuate a list, and practice the skills of categorizing, classifying, sequencing, and listing. In addition, students create their own A-to-Z shopping lists and work with food labels to create a poster entitled "Dinner for a Friend."

Book Introduction

Step 1: Say to students, "Today's book is about going shopping and all the things we can buy. Tell me about a time when you've gone shopping." Listen carefully to each student's experience.

Step 2: Spike It. Say to students, "Let's pretend we are going shopping and can buy anything we want. Now think. When I say the words 'On my shopping trip I am going to buy...,' what words can you use to complete the sentence?"

Step 3: Record the words on chart paper or on an overhead using Spike It, as illustrated in Chapter 2. (These words need to be retrieved at a later time.) Continue to probe for vocabulary words. You may need to "move" students out of toy stores and into grocery, appliance, and clothing stores. Remember, as you record each student's response, write the word(s), point to the word(s), and say the word(s) aloud with the students.

Step 4: Show the students the book. As you read the title, author, and illustrator aloud, point out each word. Ask students, "What is the same about the author and illustrator's names?" Next, ask students to

name some of the items illustrated on the cover. Lastly, ask students to make predictions about why the book is titled *On Market Street*. Write each student's initials next to his or her prediction. When you are finished writing the predictions, turn to the title page and then the verso, and point out the book's copyright date, publisher, and dedication.

Step 5: Read the book aloud to the children, using all the dramatics you can muster. Use your voice to make the shopping trip exciting! Make sure all the students get a good look at all the illustrations.

Since students will easily pick up on the fact that the items are listed alphabetically, you may wish to ask for predictions about what item might be next. (However, with books that are not lists, it's generally a good idea to read the book through once before "working" with it.)

Step 6: Ask students to react to the book. (Don't forget to extend your wait time.) You may wish to ask students which illustration they like the best and why or how they think the cat might use some of the items the boy bought for it. Next, check the list of predictions about why the book was entitled *On Market Street*. Ask students to rename the book using a street name from their own city or town.

Step 7: Reread the book, pointing out each word. Ask students what they think a merchant is. This term is more common in Britain, although we sell "merchandise" in the United States. Ask students how the word *wonders* is used in the beginning text. Also, you may wish to ask students how the use of the word *wonders* in the book differs from its use in the following sentence: Joe wonders if it will rain tomorrow.

In addition, call attention to the plural endings of the words. Say and show some of the words in singular form and compare them to the plural forms. As you read the book as a group, use your voice to cue predictable rhyming words in the beginning and ending text. You also may wish to stop and ask students how the *X* used in Christmas tree makes the word an abbreviation.

Structure Recognition

Step 1: Begin by masking rhyming words such as *doors, stores, eye,* and *buy* in the text. Let students predict these words as they read the text as a group. Also, use "stickees" to cover the uppercase letters in the illustrations. Have students come up to the book and write the uppercase letters on the stickees. After each letter is printed, remove it and stick it next to the printed uppercase letter on the page. Next, compare and contrast the uppercase letter with the lowercase letter on each page. Finally, display the words from the student-generated Spike It list. Have students circle any words on the list that also appear in the book.

Step 2: With the students, read through all the words from the Spike It list and create a Wall of Words chart. Have students copy the list in their learning logs. Next, give students pieces of oaktag on which they may copy their "personal" words. These words can then be placed in their adopt-a-word bags.

Step 3: Because *On Market Street* is a list-and-sequence book, you will naturally focus students' attention on the list of items presented in the book rather than on any detailed plot or character study. To help students recognize the structure of *On Market Street*, begin by asking them to list examples of different kinds of food. Write the examples on chart paper in the order in which they are given. Next, ask students to list examples of different kinds of animals. Finally, repeat the exercise by asking students to list all the items in the book. (Save these lists for use in Step 4.)

Ask students to contrast the three lists. Explain to students that regardless of the differences, all three are lists.

On an alphabet chart, point out that at the beginning of the boy's shopping trip he bought items that began with the letters *a, b, c, d, e, f, g, h,* and *i.* In the middle of his shopping trip, he bought items that began with the letters *j, k, l, m, n, o, p, q, r, s,* and *t.* Finally, at the end of his shopping trip, he bought items that began with the letters *u, v, w, x, y,* and *z.* The shopping trip had a beginning, middle, and end just as the book and story have a beginning, middle, and end—it had a sequence just as

the alphabet has a sequence, with a beginning, middle, and end.

Finally, tell the students to pretend that the boy has asked them to go shopping with him on Market Street. Ask them to name some items they'd buy at the beginning of the shopping trip, in the middle, and at the end. Record this shopping trip on an audiotape and play it back for the students.

Step 4: During Step 4 you may wish to do some of the following:

- Reinforce beginning consonant sounds.
- Point out the commas behind each listed item. Practice punctuating a list.
- Have students point out words with double-letter combinations, such as *apples, books, eggs, lollipops, noodles, ribbons, umbrellas, trees,* and *zippers.*
- Count the number of gloves and decide how many pairs there are.
- Read the different clocks to tell the time. Ask students how many times the clock in the middle of the woman's forehead would chime during the school day if it chimed every hour. How many times would it chime while they slept?
- Name the different musical instruments in the illustration.
- Count the pairs of shoes.
- Speculate on how many apple pies the woman could bake with all the apples she has.
- Have students categorize items from the book under the following labels: Things to Eat, Things to Wear.
- Scramble the items students listed in Step 3 (words with pictures are handy). Have students classify the items by providing the appropriate category labels.

Step 5: Now students should retell the story as a group. However, instead of asking students to recall all of the items listed in *On Market Street,* read the opening rhyming text together as a group. Next, have students take turns naming something the group would buy on their own shopping trip. Have students use the pointer and the alphabet chart. (You may even wish to record their ideas on chart paper for creating an all-class Big Book at a later time.)

Language Immersion

TO MARKET, TO MARKET!

MATERIALS NEEDED: grocery-, department-, and discount-store newspaper ads; grocery- and department-store bags; cash receipts; food labels; art supplies.

OBJECTIVE: Working in small groups, students will use newspaper ads to create a shopping list of items that begin with the different letters of the alphabet.

    1. Students cut items ranging from *a* to *z* out of the ads, then label and arrange them in list fashion.

    2. Anything not found in the ads can be drawn on the list and labeled.

    3. Each group stands and orally identifies its listed items.

    4. Lists are displayed in the room along with cash-register receipts and shopping bags.

REINFORCEMENT: Send a letter home encouraging each family to compile a list of household items with the initial letters *a* through *z*.

OTHER BOOKS: Other Caldecott books you can use with newspaper ads to reinforce the alphabet, initial sounds, counting, colors, and shapes include *Alphabetics, Jambo Means Hello, Color Zoo, Ten, Nine, Eight, Hosie's Alphabet,* and *Ape in a Cape.*

TIME TO EAT!

OBJECTIVE: Working individually, each student will create a poster by selecting from different food labels those foods he or she would choose to serve as a meal for a friend.

    1. Each student selects from food labels the foods he or she would want to serve a friend.

    2. Each student pastes these items on a poster entitled "Dinner for a Friend" and prints the name of each item.

    3. Each student conferences with another student, and then in groups of four. Add teacher conferences, if desired.

4. Each student shows his or her poster to the class and describes the items he or she has chosen.

5. Posters are displayed around the room.

REINFORCEMENT: Send a letter home encouraging the following activity: Each family member chooses his or her favorite food items. Labels of each item are saved and displayed on the refrigerator until all are collected. (After the project is done, each family sends the labels to school to replenish the label supply for the language-immersion activity.)

OTHER BOOKS: Other Caldecott books suitable for the above activity include *Stone Soup, Rain Makes Applesauce, Mice Twice,* and *May I Bring a Friend?*

Strega Nona

Big Anthony disobeyed Strega Nona's orders not to touch the magic pasta pot and now he's got a BIG pasta problem! But Strega Nona knows how to let the punishment fit the crime.

With this cheerfully illustrated book from Tomie dePaola, students review sight vocabulary words, identify contractions, and practice punctuating dialogue and doubling final consonants when adding the suffixes *-ing* and *-ed*. In addition to cause-effect and problem-solution thinking, students also create an SWBS chart and use synectics to nurture their creativity. Finally, students use their imaginations not only to create original pasta poems but also to create a little magic of their own.

Book Introduction

Step 1: Say to students, "Today's book is about a magic pasta pot— a pot that magically cooks spaghetti! Now, in real life when we cook spaghetti—or pasta, as it is called in this story—we don't have a magic pot to do it for us. So tell me about a time you either helped cook pasta or ate pasta."

Step 2: Spike It. Ask students, "When I say, 'Pasta is…,' what words can you use to complete the sentence?" Probe for vocabulary describing how pasta tastes and the different kinds of pasta and what each looks like.

Step 3: Record the words on chart paper or on an overhead. (These words will be especially helpful when students write their pasta poems later during language immersion.)

Step 4: Show students the book and state the title and author-illustrator. Explain that dePaola wrote the words for the book and did the illustrations as well. Ask students, "What do the words from the cover 'an old tale retold' mean?" Ask students, "Can you name other examples of old tales, such as *Cinderella* and *Rumpelstiltskin*?" Ask students to view

the cover art and make predictions about the kind of person Strega Nona is. Write these predictions on the board or chart paper with each student's initials.

Step 5: Read the book aloud without stopping. This allows students to hear the dialogue and follow the story sequence.

Step 6: Ask students to react to the book. Check the students' predictions about the character of Strega Nona. (This may lead to a discussion of character traits. Encourage students to cite examples from the story to support their opinions of Strega Nona.)

Step 7: Read the story as a group. All students should join in on repetitions such as *headaches, husbands*, and *warts*, as well as the magic chants. Use your voice to cue words. For example, let students supply the words *shouted* and *bubbling* as you read the sentence "Big Anthony rushed in and shouted the magic words again; but the pot kept bubbling."

Pose the following question: "I have a penny in my hand. Let's pretend it's a magic penny that can perform one magical feat—one time only. In other words, once we say the magic words, what we've asked the magic penny to do will happen, but the magic will be gone forever. But in order to make it magical, we must decide and agree what its only magical power will be. Now think. Tell us what one magical thing you would want the penny to do and why."

After discussion, you might want to ask the students to list practical ways of accomplishing the magical wishes they listed above because, after all, magical pennies don't exist. (It's helpful to identify the wishes as "goals" and the suggestions as "ways to reach the goal.")

Structure Recognition

Step 1: Read the story together as a group while you mask different words and sentences. Help students with particularly difficult vocabulary words, such as *compliments, potions*, and *barricade*. One technique to help reinforce these words is to write the new or difficult word in a box and ask students to generate synonyms for it. Using this technique,

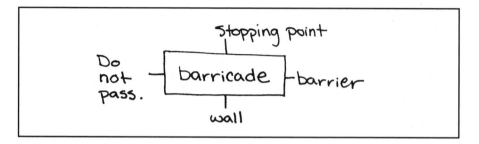

students link their known vocabulary words to new words.

Next, have students mark any words from their Spike It list that also appear in the story. (Note: The words generated during this particular Spike It exercise will be more valuable later during the writing activity, so don't let the lack of matches lead students to believe they've failed. All of their efforts are useful contributions to their literacy development!)

Step 2: With the students, read all the words from the Spike It exercise and create a wall of words chart. Have students write the words in their learning logs.

Step 3: Demonstrate cause and effect to the students by banging a wooden spoon on the bottom of an empty cooking pot. Then ask the students the following questions:
- What caused the banging noise you just heard? (spoon hitting pot)
- When I hit the pot with the spoon, what is the effect? (noise; spoon and pot may show signs of damage)

Write on the board:
    Cause: spoon hitting pot   Effect: noise

Next, ask students to imagine they are watching a pot of water boiling on a stove. Ask the following questions:
- What causes the water to boil? (heat)
- What effect does the heat from the stove have on the water? (water boils, steam rises from pot)

Write on the board:
    Cause: heat from stove   Effect: water boils, steam rises

76

Finally ask students to recall the story Strega Nona. Ask the students the following questions:

◆ What caused the pasta pot to make pasta? (magic spells)
◆ What effect did the spells have on the pasta pot? (one made pot boil; one made pot stop boiling)

Write on the board:

    Cause: magic spells   Effect: one spell made pot boil
                                       one spell made pot stop boiling

Next, demonstrate problem solution to students. Tell the students that they are going to help you solve a problem. Then say, "It is raining outside, and I am getting wet. What's my problem and how can I solve it?" Write the students' ideas on the board. A sample listing may look like this:

        The Problem Is: I am getting wet
    Some Solutions Are: come inside, get a raincoat, use an umbrella,
   The Solution I Choose: come inside
      I do the Solution: I walk inside to come out of the rain

Next, say, "I broke my pencil, and now I can't finish my work. What's my problem and how can I solve it?" Write the students' ideas on the board. A sample listing may look like this:

        The Problem Is: I can't finish work with broken pencil
    Some Solutions Are: use a pen, borrow a pencil, don't complete work
   The Solution I Choose: borrow a pencil
      I Do the Solution: I ask a friend for a pencil

Say, "Strega Nona also had a problem, because Big Anthony disobeyed her." Ask the following:

◆ What was Strega Nona's problem? (couldn't sleep in her own bed because her house was filled with pasta)
◆ What was Strega Nona's solution to her problem? (Big Anthony ate all the pasta)
◆ Why did Strega Nona choose this solution? (let punishment fit the crime)
◆ How did Strega Nona carry out her solution? (gave Big Anthony

fork)

◆ What effect did Strega Nona's solution to her problem have on Big Anthony? (made Big Anthony ill, taught him a lesson, etc.)

Step 4: As you reread the book, you may wish to do some of the following:

◆ Review basic sight vocabulary used in the story. Write original sentences using sight vocabulary words.

◆ Have students point to all contractions.

◆ Have students say the words that make up the contractions and then recite the letters, including the apostrophe, of each contraction.

◆ Have students do Punctuation Punch-Out. Have students write original dialogue and punctuate it correctly.

◆ Point out the unusual structure in the following sentence: "Out of the windows and through the doors came the pasta and the pot kept right on bubbling." Have students practice writing sentences using this sentence structure.

◆ Point out the *j* sound for *g* in *magic*. Have students identify other words with this same letter-sound pattern.

◆ Point out the use of the suffixes *-ful* in *wonderful*, *-ment* in *punishment*, and *-able* in *valuable*. Have students write additional words using those suffixes.

◆ Point out the spelling rule used in *getting*, *beginning*, and *grabbed*. (Double the final consonant if the word has one syllable, is accented on the last syllable, or ends in a single consonant preceded by a single vowel.) Practice spelling these three words.

Step 5: Before you begin the group retelling of *Strega Nona*, prepare an SWBS chart with your students. Explain the chart and ask students to supply the SOMEBODY, WANTED, BUT, SO information. Your chart may look similar to the one below:

S(SOMEBODY): Big Anthony

W(WANTED): Wanted to impress everyone with the magic pasta pot

B(BUT): But he didn't pay attention so he doesn't know how to stop the pot

S(SO):   Strega Nona stops the pot and makes Big Anthony eat all the extra pasta

Leave the SWBS chart on the board to help students recall the story. Begin the group retelling and continue as each student holds the book and tells a small portion of the story.

Language Immersion

PASTA POEMS

OBJECTIVE: Individually or with a partner, each student will create an original pasta poem.

1. Use the following synectics exercise to prepare students before writing. Ask students to jot down their ideas (answers) to the following questions:

- How is food like a suitcase?
- Pretend you are the refrigerator in your house. What do you see, hear, smell, and feel?
- Give examples of a food that is good and one that is bad.

After each question, record some of the unique answers on chart paper.

2. Have students gather around a display of different types of pasta. Make sure the students are able to touch the pasta and read the labels. Say the names of each pasta aloud with the students. If possible, show magazine pictures of the different pastas used in prepared dishes.

3. Read the words from the Wall of Words chart together as a group.

4. As a group, write a poem. Use the ones below as models:

> Stringy linguini
> Is the favorite of Mimi's,
> Spaghetti is preferred by Spot.
> But I like vermicelli
> To fill up my belly.
> I can eat at least 100 pots!

Eddie likes spaghetti.
But Poodles likes noodles.
I like mine cold. He likes his hot.
Here it comes, tummy,
Ready or not!

5. Students create poems.

6. Students conference first in pairs and then in groups of four. (Add formal teacher conferences, if desired.)

7. Students write final drafts of poems on lined paper. The final drafts are pasted on construction paper and decorated with different kinds of pasta. All poems are displayed around the room.

8. Students record their poems on audiotape and prepare a simple Pasta Poem booklet. Both are kept in the listening library for future student use.

MATERIALS NEEDED: a display of packages of different kinds of pasta with each pasta's name clearly visible, art supplies, magazine pictures of different pasta dishes.

REINFORCEMENT: Send a letter home encouraging this activity: While at the grocery store with their families, students read all the names of the different kinds of pasta.

OTHER BOOKS: Other Caldecott books you may wish to use as a basis for student poetry writing include *In the Forest, Song and Dance Man, Ten, Nine, Eight, Hide and Seek Fog, King Bidgood's in the Bathtub, Marshmallow*, and *Frederick.*

IMAGINING

OBJECTIVE: Each student will create a poster of one magical toy, appliance, tool, etc., that only he or she controls. The poster will include the magical words that start and stop the object.

1. Provide students with art supplies and explain the learning objective.

2. Students draw their magical object and write the magic words or

spell beneath it.

3. Each student conferences with another student and then in groups of four. Each student makes any changes necessary. (Add formal teacher conference, if desired.)

4. Students present their posters to the class. Students say the magic words or chants and then describe what their magical object can do.

5. Students' posters are displayed around the room.

REINFORCEMENT: Send a letter home encouraging each family to draw a magical object that helps each member of the family in some way. A "spell" can be written too. Handle this well so parents don't think you're encouraging the use of magic. The REAL magic you want students to use is their imaginations!

OTHER BOOKS: Other Caldecott books appropriate for the above activity include *The Amazing Bone, Sylvester and the Magic Pebble, The Talking Eggs, Saint George and the Dragon, Rumpelstiltskin, Duffy and the Devil, Alexander and the Wind-Up Mouse,* and *The Magic Finger.*

Where the Wild
Things Are

Why Mosquitoes Buzz
in People's Ears

Where the Wild Things Are

Every child "makes mischief," and Max is no exception in Maurice Sendak's classic *Where the Wild Things Are*. While enjoying this book, students create monsters while writing a Big Book, sequence events, answer questions that require inferencing skills, practice the phonics skill of the *s* sound for *c*, and create original travel brochures describing Max's very own Paradise Island.

Book Introduction

Step 1: Say to students, "Today's book is about taking an imaginary trip. Everybody has imagined taking a trip. Tell me about a time you've taken a trip—it can be a real trip or a trip you've imagined."

Next, say to students, "Today's book is also about some wonderful imaginary monsters. Everybody has thought about monsters at one time or another. Tell me about some monsters you've imagined."

Step 2: Spike It. Ask students, "When I say the words 'My trip was...,' what words can you use to complete the sentence?"

Next, ask students, "When I say the words 'Monsters are...,' what words can you use to complete the sentence?"

Steps 3 and 4: Record their answers and continue to probe. Then introduce the book's front matter and ask for predictions.

Step 5: Sendak's book lends itself especially well to a book orchestration. For *Where the Wild Things Are* include the following steps:

◆ Read the book aloud to your students, using an opaque projector so the room is slightly dark.
◆ As you read, play Grieg's "Peer Gynt Suite 1: The Hall of the Mountain King." (Check your local library's music collection.)
◆ As you read, crescendo your voice where the text states, "Let the rumpus begin!"

- Let the "rumpus" music of the suite play while you show the "rumpus" illustrations.
- Stop the music abruptly when Max says, "Now stop!" and finish reading the book.

Step 6: Ask students to react to the book and then check predictions.

Step 7: Help students with the words *mischief, private, rumpus,* and *gnashed.* Draw students' attention to the book's wonderful language use and rhythm, as in "An ocean tumbled by" and "He sailed off through night and day and in and out of weeks and almost over a year...." Ask students the following questions:

- "Read" the picture on page 10. What are some emotions Max is feeling at this time?
- Compare Max's command to the wild things after the rumpus to the command he'd received from his mother.
- How do we know that Max never really left his room—that this was an imaginary trip?

Structure Recognition

Steps 1 and 2: Reread the book using cloze procedure and ask students to circle any words on the Spike It lists that also appear in the book. Then have students choose words from the Spike It list, first for the Wall of Words, then for their learning logs or word bags.

Step 3: Begin by demonstrating sequencing. First, have one student describe what he or she did from the time he or she got up in the morning until the time he or she arrived at school. As the student recounts the events, list them on the board in a column with the student's name at the top. Next, ask another student to recount his or her morning and list the events in a second column.

Have the students compare and contrast the lists. Erase any differences in the two lists. With the students, number the remaining events as first, second, third, fourth, etc. Explain that this numbered list is a sequence of events.

With the students, create a chart that lists in order the events in *Where the Wild Things Are.* Display this chart in the room and label it *Sequence of Events.*

Step 4: As you reread the book, you may wish to do some of the following:

◆ Have students act out the following passage: "roared their terrible roars, gnashed their terrible teeth, rolled their terrible eyes and showed their terrible claws."

◆ Point out the use of larger type with the words "Wild Thing" and "I'll eat you up!" Ask students why these words appear in larger type.

◆ Explain the phonics rule of the *c* sounding like an *s* when it is followed by the vowels *e, i,* or *y,* as in the words *ocean, ceiling,* and *once.* Practice using these words in original sentences.

◆ Other additional phonics and usage activities you may wish to include:

-the sound of *ew* in *grew.* Match the sounds and letter to words such as *threw* and *blew.*

-the use of *bye* in the word *good-bye.* Use *bye, by,* and *buy* appropriately in sentences.

-the use of *through.* Use it in original sentences along with *threw.*

Step 5: Have students take turns telling the story as a group.

Language Immersion

A MONSTER OF A BOOK!

OBJECTIVES: Students will assist the teacher in constructing a Big Book of *Where the Wild Things Are.*

1.Using their own copies of *Where the Wild Things Are,* students assist the teacher in preparing the text that will be attached to the illustrated Big Book pages. Students assist the teacher with spelling and punctuation as they check to make sure the teacher's

printed text matches the book's text exactly. (The teacher does all the printing so the text copy is uniform.)

2. The prepared text is attached to the pages. Each student selects a page and illustrates it.

3. The illustrated pages are laminated or covered with clear contact paper for protection.

4. As a group, students assemble the pages in order, and the teacher staples or binds the book.

5. The Big Book is read as a group.

6. The Big Book is "ceremoniously" placed in the classroom library.

MATERIALS NEEDED: art supplies, lined paper, clear contact paper if lamination is not available, several different copies of travel brochures (the kinds of brochures found at travel agencies and state and city tourist-information centers), large paper suitable for creating a Big Book.

REINFORCEMENT: Send home a three- or four-page stapled booklet. Encourage each family to create a story, with each member of the family contributing a line or two.

OTHER BOOKS: Almost any book is suitable for transforming into a Big Book. However, some that especially lend themselves include *Bear Party, The House That Jack Built, Have You Seen My Duckling?, Lon Po Po, Swimmy,* and *The Happy Day.*

Note: Check into purchasing computer software that prints students' original stories in Big Book size. Using this software can ease the burden of printing so many books by hand.

MAX'S ISLAND TRAVEL BROCHURE

OBJECTIVE: Individually or in pairs, students will create a travel brochure that advertises "Max's Paradise Island."

1. Supply each student with copies of two different travel brochures.

2. Have students as a large group identify the similarities or common features of the brochures. List the common features on the board or on chart paper.

Some common features might include:
- Name of island (For this example, an island is used; however, the brochures are more likely to deal with campgrounds, amusement parks, etc.)
- Location of island (A map is sometimes included)
- What island looks like (A description)
- Who or what lives on the island, what they look like, and how they act (A picture is usually included)
- A list of things to do on the island

3. Using some or all of the above features as guidelines, students create a brochure describing a trip to Max's Paradise Island.

4. Students conference with other students in pairs and then in groups of four. (Add formal teacher conferences, if desired.)

5. Students present their brochures to the class.

6. All brochures are displayed.

REINFORCEMENT: Send a letter home explaining the language-extension activity the students just completed. Encourage parents to pick up all kinds of brochures for their child to read. The child can keep the brochures and sort them according to types, places, etc.

OTHER BOOKS: Other Caldecott books appropriate for the above activity include *Hey, Al, The Angry Moon, Polar Express, Arrow to the Sun, The Glorious Flight: Across the Channel with Louis Blériot,* and *Wheel on the Chimney.*

Why Mosquitoes
Buzz in People's Ears

Students will delight in the rich language and wonderful cadence of this West African tale boldly illustrated by Leo and Diane Dillon. Students demonstrate cause and effect, use powerful verbs in original sentences, create their own "sound" words, and work cooperatively to act out the story.

Book Introduction

Step 1: Say to students, "Today's book is about animals that live in the jungle. Tell me about some jungle animals you've seen in the zoo, on television, or in books."

Steps 2 and 3: Spike It. Ask students, "When I say, 'Some jungle animals are...,' what words can you use to complete the sentence?" Record their answers and continue to probe.

Step 4: When introducing this book, use a world map to show students where West Africa is. Also, read from the introduction of Gail E. Haley's *A Story A Story,* which explains the significance of the repetition of words ("Africans repeat words to make them stronger"). Haley also provides the traditional introductory words that begin all African tales. Introduce the book's front matter and ask for predictions.

Step 5: To bring this story alive and make it as entertaining as possible, practice reading the story several times before reading it to students. Practice will help make the "sound" words (*mek, krik,* etc.) a real part of each animal's character.

Step 6: Ask students to react to the book and then check predictions.

Step 7: Help students with the following words: *burrow, tidbit, council, timid, summons, conscience.* Make sure students join in on the

repetitive parts of the story as well as the sound words. Ask students to describe each animal's personality and to use words, phrases, and actions from the story to support their opinions. You may also want to do the following:

◆ Have students listen to several pages of the story with the sound words omitted. Then read the story with the words included. Ask students, "Which version is better and why?"

◆ Ask, "In general, what can we say about all of the animals' actions leading up to the owlet's death?"

◆ Ask, "What other animals are pesky, like the mosquito, and probably deserve a 'KPAO!'?"

Structure Recognition

Steps 1 and 2: Reread the book using cloze procedures and ask students to circle words on the Spike It list that also appear in the book. Then have students choose words from the Spike It list, first for the Wall of Words, then for their learning logs or word bags.

Step 3: Begin by demonstrating cause and effect to the students. Say, "Pretend for a moment that a swarm of mosquitoes has just invaded the classroom and several have landed on your arms and legs. The mosquitoes' bites sting. What do you do to make the mosquitoes stop biting you at this very moment?" (Replies: slap mosquitoes, run around room, leave room)

Next, say, "The mosquitoes are gone, and your bites are healed. We're all back to normal. Now tell me: What effect did the mosquitoes' bites have on you? In other words, what did the bites cause you to do?" Write responses on the board, similar to this:

Effect: slap at mosquitoes, run around room, leave room

Next, say, "What was the cause of your slapping and running and leaving?" Write responses on the board, similar to this:

Cause: mosquitoes' bites, buzzes

Summarize by saying, "In other words, a mosquito and its bite

caused you to slap your skin, run around the room, and/or try to leave the room. This is an example of cause and effect."

Next, draw the students' attention to a display of dominoes. The dominoes should be arranged so that when the first one is pushed over, a chain reaction results and the remaining dominoes fall over in succession.

Demonstrate the "domino effect" and ask students to explain how cause and effect worked in the demonstration.

Ask students to draw an analogy between the demonstration with the dominoes and what happened in the story.

Step 4: As you reread the book, you may wish to do some of the following:

♦ Ask students to explain in their own words the following expressions:
   -The iguana says to "try me" when the mosquito says he has seen something the iguana will never believe.
   -The crow goes to "spread the alarm."
   -Mother Owl says she cannot "bear to wake the sun."
   -King Lion accuses Rabbit of breaking a "law of nature."
   -Rabbit says he was "minding my own business" when Python chased him out of his home.

♦ Since the sound words in this story are exceptional, ask students to use their imaginations and create other sound words to accompany other animals. (What sound word would go well with a kangaroo?)

♦ Draw the students' attention to words ending in -*ed* and -*ing*, especially the following: *lumbered, startled, alarmed, demanded, annoyed, bounded, scurried; prowling, leaping, screeching, flapping, slithering*.

♦ Read the sentences from the book that contain the above words. Ask students to substitute other verbs. After reading the sentence aloud with the substitute verb, ask how using a different word changed the meaning. (For example, substitute *crawling* for *slithering*.)

♦ Have students use the above words in original sentences.

Step 5: Have students take turns telling the story as a group.

Language Immersion

FOLLOW THE "FAULT LINE"

MATERIALS NEEDED: a roll of newsprint, art supplies, audiotape recorder, video camera recorder (optional).

OBJECTIVE: In small groups, students create a "fault line" that describes each animal's actions and its effect on the next animal. Students begin with the mosquito.

    1.Introduce the concept of an illustrated story map by briefly telling the story of the Three Little Pigs and drawing the illustrations and arrows, then writing a brief description beneath each illustration. (Remember: If you're not artistic, do the best you can. That's what you ask of your students!)

    2. Provide each small group with a long strip of newsprint (newspapers sell their end rolls cheaply).

    3. State the learning objective.

    4. Explain the process as follows:

    - Begin the fault line with the mosquito.

    - Draw a picture of the mosquito and describe its actions underneath.

    - Proceed with the fault line until the final action (owlet's death).

    5. After the fault lines are completed, display the strips along the walls at student eye level. Have groups of students walk by and read one another's presentations.

REINFORCEMENT: Send a letter home explaining how cause and effect were used in class. Encourage each family to find simple, everyday instances of cause and effect. For example, when the light switch is turned on, what happens? When the water faucet is turned off, what happens?

OTHER BOOKS: Other Caldecott books that would lend themselves to story maps include *It Could Always Be Worse, Finders Keepers, One Fine Day, Once a Mouse...*, and *The Bremen-Town Musicians.*

ACTING OUT

OBJECTIVE: Working as a group, students select parts, prepare the script, and perform *Why Mosquitoes Buzz in People's Ears.*

    1. A four-part planning process prepares students to accomplish the learning objective.

    a) Write the learning objective in the middle of the chalkboard.

    b) Have four different pieces of chart paper around the objective with the following headings:

> Our Final Goal
> Things We Need
> Steps to Follow
> Problems to Solve

    c) Ask students to explain the educational objective in their own words. Check for understanding.

    d) Have students brainstorm ideas to complete the four steps in the planning process, first in small groups, then as a large group.

    e) Have students reach a consensus during the planning process.

    f) Leave the process steps displayed during the completion of the language-immersion activity.

    2. Students identify the speaking parts and agree on who will perform each part. Students also select a narrator who will stand at the side of the performance. Finally, students select people for the chorus who will narrate the sound words as a group.

    3. Students prepare their scripts by highlighting their individual parts with colored markers. (Obtain permission from the book's publisher to word-process the text and duplicate it for student use.)

    4. Rehearse the play, using an audiotape recorder to let students, especially the chorus, hear how they sound. (An audiotape during final rehearsals can be made and kept in the listening library.)

    5. Videotape the final performance. If the class is a large one, divide into two groups and have two separate performances. Play to each student's strength. For example, allow students who dislike performing to direct, create simple props and sets, and run the VCR.

REINFORCEMENT: Send a letter home encouraging each family to have a "group read" by selecting a story in which each family member can read a different character's lines. (Suggest some books and allow students to check these books out of the classroom library.)

OTHER BOOKS: Other Caldecotts that can be acted out or performed as Readers' Theater or choral reading include *Goldilocks and the Three Bears, Lon Po Po, Frederick, Five Little Monkeys, Fables, Mirandy and Brother Wind, If All the Seas Were One Sea, Drummer Hoff, A Story A Story,* and *The Judge.*

Freight Train

Make Way for Ducklings

Freight Train

U sing fewer than 60 words, and illustrations that seem to move right off the page, Donald Crews speeds your students cross-country in *Freight Train*. But don't let the lack of words mislead you—a whole lot of learning lies deep within this book. First, students create a comparison poem using joggers or runners in the same way Crews uses the freight train. In addition, students have great fun making up silly rhymes as they travel by train to visit Dr. Seuss! Consequently, it's not the number of words in a book that counts but what you do with them!

Book Introduction

Step 1: Say to students, "Today's book is about a freight train. A freight train doesn't carry people, except for the people who run the train. What do you think a freight train carries if it doesn't carry people? Tell me about a time you've seen a freight train. If you haven't seen one in person, think about a time you've seen one on television, in a book, or in a magazine or newspaper."

Step 2: Spike It. Ask students, "When I say the words 'A freight train is...,' what words can you use to complete the sentence?"

Steps 3 and 4: Record their answers and continue to probe. Then introduce the book's front matter and ask for predictions.

Step 5: You can add excitement and interest to your first reading of *Freight Train* if you include the sound of a train and its whistle. Almost any sound-effects record includes a whistling train. However, if you can't get a record, try borrowing a train whistle. Pull it out of your pocket as you read the last page of the story and "signal" that the freight train is indeed "gone."

Step 6: Ask students to react to the book and then check their predictions.

Step 7: Read the book as a group, helping students with the words *caboose, hopper, gondola,* and *tender*. (You may wish to use other resource materials to help students understand the function of each of these train cars.) Also, you can help students understand the word *trestle* by showing them several pictures of bridges. (The bridge is the top of the tree, but the trestle is the trunk.) Also, ask students to imagine what is inside the tank, hopper, and box cars. In addition, ask students where they think the freight train came from and where it is going. Finally, before this first group reading of the book, prepare labeled paper train cars in their appropriate colors. As you read the story with the group, assemble the paper train on the wall behind you. Leave this train displayed for future student reference and scrounging.

Structure Recognition

Steps 1 and 2: Reread the book using cloze procedures. Next, have students choose words from the Spike It list, first for the Wall of Words, then for their learning logs and word bags.

Step 3: *Freight Train* is a very simplified version of the general-statement-and-elaboration structure. From the very simple concept of the freight train, the author elaborates through the use of precise words and "moving" illustrations. You can help students understand this structure by completing the following exercise or one similar to it. Begin with the following categories listed on the board or on chart paper:

Title of Book: *Bear*
Naming (Subject)   **Telling** (Predicate)

Explain to your students that you will begin with a subject, or a "naming" part, of a sentence and that they are to elaborate or add details to the subject, one detail at a time. The naming category could look something like this as the elaboration grows:

The bear
The brown bear

The cute brown bear
The cute brown bear with the blue eyes
The cute brown bear with blue eyes and a yellow vest

Next, explain to students that they need to complete the predicate, or "telling" part, of the sentence. The telling category could look something like this:

is eating
is eating blueberry pie
is eating blueberry pie with ice cream
is eating blueberry pie with ice cream at his grandmother's house
is eating blueberry pie with ice cream at his grandmother's house
    on a Sunday afternoon

So from the general statement or concept of *bear* came the following elaborated sentence:

The cute brown bear with blue eyes and a yellow vest is eating blueberry pie with ice cream at his grandmother's house on a Sunday afternoon.

Next, have students examine their copies of *Freight Train*. Ask them to list the details that describe the freight train and then list the "telling part" of the story that tells what the freight train did.

Naming
Example: Red caboose at the back
        Orange tank car next
        Yellow hopper car
        Green cattle car
        Blue gondola car
        Purple box car
        Black tender and a Black steam engine

Telling
Example: Going through tunnels
        Going by cities
        Crossing trestles
        Moving in darkness

Moving in daylight
Going, going
Gone

Record these and ask students to explain how the two story structures (*Bear* and *Freight Train*) are similar.

Step 4: As you reread the book, you may wish to do some of the following:

◆ Count the number of words in the entire book.
◆ Read the book using different color words.
◆ Write the book's phrases as sentences and display them on an overhead. Read this new version of the book and ask students how changing the phrases to sentences changes the rhythm of the book. (The train doesn't seem to go as fast!)
◆ Ask students the following questions:
"If you were the train tracks underneath the freight train, what would you say to the train?"
"If all the trains running today were freight trains like the one in this book, how would that affect our environment?"
"How do you know from looking at the book's illustrations that the train is moving very fast?"

Step 5: To add interest during the group retelling of the story, you may wish to have students line up according to the color of their clothing. Students could then read the text from an overhead or chart paper as they slowly chug around the room. Finally, they could be "going, going, gone" right out the classroom door and into recess, if you time it just right!

Language Immersion

RUNNERS

MATERIALS NEEDED: a world map or globe, drawing paper, art supplies.

OBJECTIVE: As a large group, students will create a poem, using *Freight*

Train as a model.

    1. Begin by having students do the following synectics exercise. Ask students to respond to the following questions/statements:

- "How is a freight train like a person who runs (a runner)?"
- "Pretend you are the shoes of a runner. What would you see, hear, smell, taste, and feel?"
- "Describe something that can run slowly."

Record students' responses on the board or chart paper.

    2. Display the text of *Freight Train* as a visual reminder.

    3. As a group, write a poem based on the model. For example:

        Runners run along this road.
        A lady with red hair
        A man with an orange cap
        A lady with a yellow shirt
        Runners.
        Running fast
        Running through tunnels
        Running in cities
        Running across bridges
        Running in the darkness
        Running in daylight
        Running, running
        Away!

Note: Be flexible. The poem does not have to match the model but should instead reflect the essence of the structure and language rhythm.

    4. Have the class read the poemlike text aloud as you record it on an audiotape. Use sound effects, if possible. Place the tape, along with the copy of the poem, in the listening library.

REINFORCEMENT: Send a letter home with the titles of several poetry books that families can check out of the library. Include a packet entitled "A Poem a Day Helps the Language Stay!" in which you've included several poems—enough for a new poem to go up on the refrigerator door every day for a week.

OTHER BOOKS: Other Caldecott books appropriate for the above activity include *Ten, Nine, Eight, Drummer Hoff, Frederick,* and *Bartholomew and the Oobleck.*

TRAVELING TO DR. SEUSS!

OBJECTIVE: Each student will create a rhyming sentence and draw a picture to illustrate it.

1. Explain to students that they are going to pretend they are train engineers, and they've gotten an urgent message from Dr. Seuss! Of course, traveling to get to where Dr. Seuss is will be quite a ride since Dr. Seuss likes all kinds of silly rhymes! (If your students are not familiar with Dr. Seuss books, now might be a good time to read some to them if you haven't already. *McElligot's Pool* is a Caldecott Honor book that is very imaginative and creative. Also, the non-Caldecott book *Marvin K. Mooney* has lots of silly made-up rhyming words that might be useful for this activity.

2. Put the following sentences on chart paper:

> The train went through snow and arrived in Tokyo.
> The train went through rain and arrived in Spain.
> The train went through dew and arrived in Timbuktu.
> The train went through air and arrived in Zaire.

Have students repeat the sentences as you point out the cities and countries on a world map or globe.

3. Now explain to the students that their trains are getting close to where Dr. Seuss lives and strange things may begin to happen! Use these silly sentence starters:

> The train went through spantetti and arrived in
>
> _____.
>
> The train went through goosh and arrived in
>
> _____.
>
> The train went through thniss and arrived in
>
> _____.

As the students supply the silly rhymes, ask them to describe what *spantetti, goosh,* and *thniss* look, feel, and smell like. Also, have

students point to a country or area on the globe or map where they think their rhyming cities or countries belong.

4. Next, students create their own silly rhymes using the base sentence:

> The train went through _____ and arrived in _____.

Students copy their sentence onto the top of a piece of drawing paper.

5. Next, students have a choice of:
- drawing their train traveling through the *thniss* or *goosh* or whatever they've created
- drawing their train arriving at the train station of their imaginary city or country
- drawing both of the above

6. As a large group presentation, each student shows his or her picture and reads his or her sentence to the class. The group may ask questions such as "What does your *goosh* feel like?" Or "Where in the world is your city of Bengetti?"

7. Display the students' pictures along some train "tracks" on the classroom wall. (You could also send some to Dr. Seuss for his enjoyment!)

REINFORCEMENT: Send home a list of Dr. Seuss books that parents can read to their children. Also, encourage parents and children to play rhyming games while waiting for stop lights or while grocery shopping. For example, at the grocery store a parent might say, "This box is red, now give me some _____." The child could answer by saying "bread."

OTHER BOOKS: Other Caldecotts appropriate for silly rhymes include *Ape in a Cape, Rain Makes Applesauce,* and *Bartholomew and the Oobleck.*

Make Way for Ducklings

Like Michael, the police officer, your students will want to see Mr. and Mrs. Mallard and their ducklings safely home in Robert McCloskey's classic *Make Way for Ducklings*. Students also problem solve, spot environmental print within the text, find their way through Boston by reading a city map, and finally, plan, organize, and execute a "Happy Duck Day!"

Book Introduction

Step 1: Say to students, "Today's book is about ducks. Tell me about a time when you've seen a duck—either a real one or a picture of one."

Steps 2, 3, and 4: Spike It. Ask students, "When I say the words 'Ducks are...,' what words can you use to complete the sentence?" Record their answers and continue to probe. Then introduce the book's front matter and ask for predictions.

Steps 5 and 6: Add a duck call and a police whistle to your reading! Ask students to react to the book and then check predictions.

Step 7: After the first group reading of the book, ask students to read the print in the illustrations, words like *tweet* and *honk* as well as the print on the license plates and store windows. Let students have fun with the rhyming names of the ducklings. Suggest that they come up with names that rhyme with Bill. Also, have students explain the term *molt* and the expression *all of a dither*. Ask the following questions:

◆ "What effect did the ducks' journey across town have on traffic?"
◆ "This book was illustrated in 1941. How can you tell?"
◆ "This was a story written and illustrated 50 years ago; why do you suppose it is still popular today?"

Structure Recognition

Steps 1 and 2: Reread the book using cloze procedures and ask students to circle words on the Spike It list that also appear in the book. Then have students choose words from the Spike It list, first for the Wall of Words, then for their learning logs.

Step 3: Since the story is based on the problem-solution structure, demonstrate the steps in problem solving. Tell the students they are going to help you solve a problem.

◆ Say, "I want to buy an ice-cream cone, but I must cross the busy street to get to the store. What is my problem, and how can I solve it?"

◆ Write the students' ideas on the board. A sample listing may look like this:

The Problem Is:	I must cross the busy street without getting hurt
Some Solutions Are:	go to the intersection, push the button to change the traffic light, and walk when the WALK light flashes; go to the intersection, look both ways, and cross when there is no traffic
The Solution I Choose:	go to the intersection, push the button to change the traffic light, and then walk when the WALK light flashes
I Do the Solution:	I follow steps above, making sure I avoid traffic
My Reasons for Choosing This Solution Are:	answers will vary

◆ Next, say, "Mrs. Mallard also had a problem in this book. What was her problem, and how was it solved?"
Problem: Mrs. Mallard had to take her ducklings safely from the island on which they were born to Public Garden, their new home
Solution: Mrs. Mallard cautiously moved through the city until

Michael, the police officer, stopped traffic long enough for Mrs. Mallard and the ducklings to cross into Public Garden

Step 4: As you reread the book, you may wish to do some of the following:

◆ Have students list all the proper nouns in the story.

◆ Ask students to act out the following sentence: "He planted himself in the center of the road, raised one hand to stop the traffic, and then beckoned with the other, the way policemen do, for Mrs. Mallard to cross over." Emphasize the phrase *beckoned with the other*.

◆ Ask students why the author uses the term *policemen* and not *police officers* in his book. (Remember: This book was first published in 1941.)

◆ Note the verb-tense shift in the last pages of the book. Change the verbs to *followed, ate, fell*, and *went*. Ask students how changing the verbs changes the meaning of the story's ending.

◆ Have students find the city of Boston on a national map.

◆ Have students identify *qu* words other than *quack*.

Step 5: Have students take turns telling the story as a group.

Language Immersion

CITY STREETS AND PLACES

MATERIALS NEEDED: several maps of Boston (the small Boston city map in a Rand-McNally Road Atlas or Massachusetts state highway map is all that is needed; information on where to obtain maps appears at the end of this activity), access to fiction and nonfiction materials about ducks.

OBJECTIVE: Given a map of Boston, students will locate the places mentioned in *Make Way for Ducklings* and plot different paths around the city.

    1. Pair students and supply each pair with a map that has been protected with contact paper or lamination film. (Stocking the

school library or media center with 15 to 20 large road atlases is an extremely worthy cause for any parent-school organization. Suggest it!)

2. Students read through *Make Way for Ducklings* and create a list of the following places: Public Garden, Beacon Hill, Beacon Street, State House, Louisburg Square, Charles River, Mount Vernon Street, Corner Book Shop, and Charles Street.

3. Using the Boston map, students locate as many of these places as possible. (Remind students that the book was written 50 years ago and that some of the areas may be "historical" in nature. An Old State House and an Old Corner Bookstore are identified on most maps, while Louisburg Square is not listed. Also, ask students to identify the Beacon Hill "district.")

4. It's very difficult to plot Mrs. Mallard's trail from her island in the Charles River back to Public Garden on a general city map of Boston. Instead, you may wish to have your students draw trails from other places in Boston back to Public Garden. For example, using a washable marker, have one group of students draw a trail from the New Charles River Dam to Public Garden while another group draws a trail from Christopher Columbus Park back to Public Garden. Next, have students write the directions in paragraph form and then explain them aloud as the other students follow along on their maps with a finger.

5. To extend this activity in another direction, obtain maps of your own city or use the city map in your local telephone book and plot different paths between various parks and public buildings. Make sure students understand and utilize the letter-number coordinates on the map.

Note: If you have difficulty obtaining maps for this or any other activity, you can order maps from the Rand-McNally Company by calling 1-800-333-0136, extension 3496.

REINFORCEMENT: Send a letter home encouraging each family to use the city map in the telephone book to locate where they live, work, grocery shop, etc.

OTHER BOOKS: Other Caldecott books appropriate for the above activity include *Madeline's Rescue, Have You Seen My Duckling?, In the Forest,* and *The Little House.*

HAPPY DUCK DAY

OBJECTIVE: Students will plan, organize, and execute activities that explore the topic of ducks.

1. As a large group, brainstorm all the possibilities for celebrating "Happy Duck Day."

2. Students divide into groups to research and execute agreed-upon areas. For example, one group could be responsible for investigating the different varieties of ducks and creating posters. Another group could rehearse and act out *Make Way for Ducklings.* Still other groups could write original duck poems and songs to be performed during the celebration and recorded "live" for the listening library.

3. In order to prepare to accomplish its goal, have each group complete a four-part planning guide. On separate pieces of paper, write the following headings:

> Our Final Goal
> Things We Need
> Steps to Follow
> Problems We Might Have

On the appropriate piece of paper, have each group:

a) State its goal

b) List any items it will need to achieve its goal

c) Identify the steps the group will need to follow to accomplish its goal and then sequence the steps from beginning to end

d) Identify any problems the group may have and suggest possible solutions or ways to avoid the problems

Post each group's planning guide.

4. Designate a time frame for research and rehearsal that fits your schedule. You may wish to research during an entire morning and "celebrate" or present during the afternoon, or you may wish to research for several days and present for an entire day.

5. Leave as much duck material as possible displayed in the room as a reminder of Happy Duck Day.

6. Have students evaluate the process of Happy Duck Day. What would they do differently, etc.? Implement these suggestions the next time you have a "Happy Day."

REINFORCEMENT: Send home a letter explaining the four-part planning process. Encourage parents to be on the lookout for any opportunities for their child to use the planning process to accomplish even small tasks, such as planning and preparing a simple meal or snack, helping plan and prepare a birthday party, etc.

OTHER BOOKS: Other Caldecott books appropriate for the above activity include *The Village of Round and Square Houses, Time of Wonder, A Tree Is Nice, The Storm Book, The Little Island, Ashanti to Zulu: African Traditions, The Desert Is Theirs, Houses from the Sea, The Glorious Flight: Across the Channel with Louis Blériot, Castle,* and *Cathedral.*

Blueberries for Sal

Frog and Toad Are Friends

Blueberries for Sal

This 1949 Caldecott Honor book by Robert McCloskey will put a smile on your students' faces as they read about the misadventures of Little Sal and Little Bear on Blueberry Hill. In addition to being a perfect example of the comparing-contrasting story structure, *Blueberries for Sal* also includes text repetition and endearing illustrations.

After reading the story, students explore cookbooks and create a recipe for their very own Blueberry Surprise! Finally, students use the cloze procedure to play blueberry black-out blocks.

Book Introduction

Step 1: Say to students, "Today's book is about two *b* words—*blueberries* and *bears*. First, tell me about a time you've eaten berries—any kind of berries."

Next, say, "Now tell me about a time you've seen a bear—either a real one or a pretend one. This bear could even be one you've seen on TV or in a magazine."

Step 2: Spike It. Ask students, "When I say the words 'Berries are...,' what words can you use to complete the sentence?"

Next, ask, "When I say the words 'Bears are...,' what words can you use to complete the sentence?"

Steps 3, 4, 5, and 6: Record their answers and continue to probe. Then introduce the book's front matter and ask for predictions. Read the book dramatically. Ask students to react to the book and then check predictions.

Step 7: As you read the book together as a group, note the repetition of many of the phrases. For example, both Little Sal and her mother as well as Little Bear and his mother were storing "food for the winter," and

both Little Sal and Little Bear "tramped" and were "tramping." You may also wish to ask students the following questions:

◆ "Why did Little Bear and his mother need to eat as many berries as they could?"

◆ "Little Sal and Little Bear thought they were following their own mothers because..."

◆ "Even though you know the copyright date of this book, what other clues can lead you to believe this book was not written and illustrated recently?"

Finally, have fun with the "sound" words such as *kuplink* and *garumpf*. Have students invent other sound words and use them in sentences.

Structure Recognition

Steps 1 and 2: Reread the book using cloze procedures and ask students to circle words on the Spike It lists that also appear in the book. Then have students choose words from the Spike It lists, first for the Wall of Words, then for their learning logs.

Step 3: *Blueberries for Sal* is an excellent example of the comparing-contrasting story structure. You can help students understand this structure by completing the following activity or one similar to it:

◆ Draw a Venn diagram on the board or on chart paper.

◆ Explain to the students that you will be using the diagram to record their ideas during a comparing-and-contrasting activity.

◆ Place an empty drinking glass and an unopened can of soup next to each other.

◆ Ask students to compare the two items (say what is the same).

◆ Record their ideas in the intersecting portion of the diagram.

◆ Ask students to contrast the two items (say what is different).

◆ Record their ideas in the opposite spheres of the diagram.

◆ Repeat the demonstration using a piece of chalk and a writing pen.

Next, ask, "How were Little Sal and Little Bear alike and how were they different while on Blueberry Hill?"

◆ Record the responses using another Venn diagram.

Finally, ask, "How were Little Sal's mother and Little Bear's mother alike and how were they different?"

◆ Record the responses using another Venn diagram.
◆ Ask students to summarize: "How did the author use comparing and contrasting in *Blueberries for Sal*?"
◆ Display both diagrams.

Step 4: As you reread the book, you may wish to do some of the following:

◆ Play Punctuation Punch-Out.
◆ Ask students why they think tin pails are no longer common household items.
◆ Ask students if they've ever canned or know anything about canning. Let them explain. (Display resource books describing canning procedures or have a guest speaker explain canning to the class.)
◆ Ask students to identify one page in the entire book that summarizes the plot of the story (page 38).
◆ Ask students to substitute words for *hustle* and *hustling* and see if the sentence meanings change.
◆ Have students practice adding *-ing* to words such as *hustle* (*e* is dropped when the ending is added).
◆ Have students practice adding endings to words where the *y* is changed to *i,* as in *hurried* and *berries.*

Step 5: Students may need to open the book and turn the pages as they retell the story. You could also practice original storytelling by creating a new story. How about a story that has a dog burying a bone in the side of a hill while on the other side of the same hill a child is burying a coin? Through a mix-up, the dog and child dig up each other's treasures.

Language Immersion

BLUEBERRY BLACK-OUT BLOCKS

MATERIALS NEEDED: pens or pencils that are close to the color of blueberries; a variety of cookbooks; magazine recipes with photos; labeled cooking utensils such as measuring cups and spoons, ladles, whisks, etc.; art supplies.

OBJECTIVE: Students supply the necessary words to create sensible meaning from a copy of the text of *Blueberries for Sal* in which words have been blacked out.

1. Supply each student with a copy of a page or two from the book that has several words blacked out. (Or have the story text word-processed and printed triple-spaced.) For example, ask students to supply the missing verbs in this segment of the text:
She picked three more berries and xxx them. Then she picked more berries and drxxxxx one in the pail—kuplunk! And the rest she xxx. Then Little Sal ate all four blueberries out of her pail!
Note: To prepare your text, refer to black-out blocks in Chapter 2.
2. Each student writes the appropriate words above the blacked-out spaces.
3. Students conference to read each other's pages and offer suggestions.
4. During the last portion of the student conference, students check their pages with the text version. Words that do not correspond exactly to the text but do not alter the meaning are not deleted. Instead, students write the text word BELOW the blacked-out word.
5. Each student reads his page aloud, pausing to allow the group to supply as many of the blacked-out words as it can. (During this large group activity, begin with the first page of the book so the entire book is read aloud.)

REINFORCEMENT: Send home a sample page of black-out blocks from the above exercise along with an explanation of how the activity helps

students create meaning. Ask parents to complete the page and then let their child "check" for meaning. Explain how parents can perform the same type of cloze activity when reading by pausing to let the child "fill in the words" as they read stories at home.

OTHER BOOKS: Almost any of the Caldecott books can be used for black-out blocks, including *The Little Island, One Fine Day, The Bremen-Town Musicians, The Talking Eggs, Little Red Riding Hood, Lon Po Po, and Gillespie and the Guards.*

BLUEBERRY SURPRISE!

OBJECTIVE: After examining different cookbooks and recipes, students write their own recipe entitled "Blueberry Surprise."

1. Distribute cookbooks to pairs of students.

2. As a large group, list some common features of the different cookbooks. For example, most cookbooks have a table of contents, an index, and an equivalents or measurement list or chart.

3. Have students select a blueberry pie or pancake recipe from a cookbook. Read three of the recipes aloud. List the common features found in the different recipes, such as a list of ingredients, directions, and cooking temperature and time. Also list some common terms, such as *beat, sift, fold,* and *stir.* Define these terms and list them on a piece of chart paper.

4. Explain the educational objective again. Explain that the students' Blueberry Surprise recipes can be anything—even spaghetti with blueberry meatballs—as long as the recipe follows the basic recipe format.

5. Students write their recipes.

6. Student pairs conference with each other.

7. Students revise and rewrite their recipes. (Include a formal teacher conference, if desired.)

8. Students draw pictures to accompany their recipes. (Show students examples from magazines that include photos and recipes.)

9. Display their recipes on classroom walls in a "Cook Nook" area that includes labeled cooking utensils, cookbooks, spices, etc.

10. After taking the recipes down, compile them in a classroom cookbook. (Display this during parent-teacher conferences or, better yet, send the cookbook home with each student and let parents write comments in the back of the book before returning it to school.)

OTHER BOOKS: Other Caldecott books appropriate for the above activity include *Mice Twice, Frederick, Stone Soup,* and *In the Night Kitchen.*

Frog and Toad Are Friends

W hat do friends do for each other? Your students will find out by reading one or all of the five stories in Arnold Lobel's delightful *Frog and Toad Are Friends*. In addition, students will use calendars to record important information, compare and contrast buttons, write letters, write an original story, and play sentence line-up.

"Spring"

Step 1: Say to students, "Today's story is about spring. Tell me how you feel when it's spring."

Steps 2, 3, and 4: Spike It. Ask students, "When I say, 'Spring is...,' what words can you use to complete the sentence?" Record their answers and continue to probe. Then introduce the book's front matter and ask for predictions.

Steps 5 and 6: Read the story dramatically. Ask students to react to the story and then check predictions.

Step 7: As you read the story together as a group, help students with the words *shutters, lying,* and *whole.*
Note the repetition of such words as *pulled, cried,* and *back.*
You may wish to ask students the following questions:

◆ "How many months had Toad been asleep?"
◆ "What date would be considered half past May?"
◆ "Have you ever wanted a friend to do something you wanted to do? What did you do to persuade him or her to go along with you?"

Structure Recognition

Steps 1 and 2: Reread the story using cloze procedures and ask students to circle words on the Spike It list that also appear in the book. Then have students choose words from the Spike It list, first for the Wall of Words, then for their learning logs.

Step 3: "Spring" is an example of the problem-solution story structure. Begin the analysis of the structure by having students complete an SWBS chart similar to the one below:

S (SOMEBODY):	Frog
W (WANTED):	Wanted Toad to wake up and enjoy spring with him
B (BUT):	But Toad wanted to sleep until mid-May
S (SO):	Frog tears off the calendar page to convince Toad it is time to wake up for spring

Leave the chart on display. Next, demonstrate problem solution to students. Explain to the students that they are going to help you solve a problem. Say, "I am writing in my journal, and I don't know how to spell a word that I want to spell correctly. What's my problem, and how can I solve it?"

Write the students' responses on the board. A sample may look like the chart below:

The Problem Is:	I want to spell a word correctly, but I'm not sure of the spelling
Some Solutions Are:	ask someone; look it up in the dictionary; see if the word is on the wall, in a book, or in my learning log
The Solution I Choose:	find the word in my learning log and also ask someone to make sure it's the right word
I Do the Solution:	I copy the word from my learning log into my journal
My Reasons for Choosing This Solution:	answers will vary

Finally, ask students to identify Frog's problem in the story "Spring" and to explain the solution. Also, ask students if they feel the solution to Frog's problem was fair to Toad. Why or why not?

Step 4: As you reread the story, you may wish to do some of the following:

◆ Practice spelling the months of the year.
◆ List all of the activities Frog had planned for Toad and himself.
◆ Practice writing the following phrases from the story as contractions: *I am, cannot, I will, we will,* and *he had.*

Step 5: Have students take turns telling the story as a group.

Language Immersion

MARK YOUR CALENDARS!

MATERIALS NEEDED: several calendars large enough to write on (insurance companies, banks, and real-estate offices are good places to get free calendars; make sure you stock up for the year—if getting commercially made calendars is not possible, have a parent volunteer make simple 16-month —September through the following year's December—calendars for you).

OBJECTIVE: Each student will mark his or her calendar according to specific directions.

1. Give each student a calendar.

2. Going month by month, have students take turns reading aloud the print on the different months of the calendar.

3. As the above process continues, have students write in important dates, such as each student's birthday, etc.

4. Give students an agenda of school dates that lists vacation days, conference days, etc. (This is where the 16-month calendar is handy.) Have students mark these dates on their calendar(s).

5. Ask students to use their calendars to answer the following

questions:
- "Which months have 31 days?"
- "How many days from today is your birthday?"
- "If Frog visited Toad on April 1, how many more days did Toad want to sleep?"
- "If the months were arranged in alphabetical order, how would the months be listed?"

Note: If you plan this activity at the beginning of the school year, your students will have school calendars with all of the important school dates marked for the rest of the year!

REINFORCEMENT: Send each student's calendar home with a letter asking parents to let their child mark the important school dates on the family calendar. Student calendars should be returned to school.

OTHER BOOKS: Other Caldecotts appropriate for the above activity include *Ox-Cart Man, The Little Island,* and *The Little House.*

"A Lost Button"

(It is recommended that "The Story" be read last because of the writing activity that accompanies it.)

Step 1: Say to students, "Today's story is about looking for a lost button. Tell me about a time you've lost something and had to look for it."

Step 2: Spike It. Ask students, "When I say, 'When I lose something, I...,' what words can you use to complete the sentence?"

Next, ask, "When I say, 'Buttons are...,' what words can you use to complete the sentence?"

Steps 3, 4, 5, and 6: Record their answers and continue to probe. Then introduce the book's front matter. Read the story dramatically. Ask students to react to the story.

Step 7: As you read the book together as a group, you may wish to record the description of Toad's button as each attribute is revealed in the story. Also, list the different animals and the buttons they found. Finally, you may wish to ask the following questions:

◆ "How do you know that at one point in the story Toad is very frustrated about finding several buttons that are not his?"
◆ "How does Toad's use of the extra buttons at the end of the story demonstrate the title of the book *Frog and Toad Are Friends?*"
◆ "Explain how the phrase *jumped for joy* is used on page 39."

Structure Recognition

Steps 1 and 2: Reread the story using cloze procedures and ask students to circle words on the Spike It lists that also appear in the book. Then have students choose words from the Spike It lists, first for the Wall of Words, then for their learning logs.

Step 3: Because "The Lost Button" provides a unique opportunity for students to practice comparing and contrasting, rather than focus on the problem-solution story structure, do the following activity instead (use a real button for this demonstration):

◆ Allow students to inspect the button.
◆ Explain that the class will be comparing and contrasting the sample button with Toad's button as it is described in the story.
◆ Draw a Venn diagram on the board.
◆ List the similarities and differences in the appropriate areas.
◆ Have students explain orally the similarities and differences between the sample button and Toad's button.
◆ As a large group, have students compose a one-sentence description of the sample button.

Step 4: As you reread the story, you may wish to do some of the following:

◆ Point out the prepositional phrases in the story. Have students

practice writing sentences with prepositional phrases.

◆ Note the sentence structure and punctuation in the following compound sentence: "Not only do my feet hurt, but I have lost one of the buttons on my jacket" (subject, verb, comma, conjunction, subject, verb). Have students practice writing compound sentences.

Step 5: Have students take turns telling the story as a group or make up a story about something lost—"The Lost Shoe," for example.

Language Immersion

BUTTON, BUTTON

MATERIALS NEEDED: several different buttons—one for each student.

OBJECTIVE: In pairs and using a Venn diagram, students will compare and contrast two different buttons. Students will then write a short paragraph describing the differences and similarities between their two buttons. Finally, students will share their paragraphs orally with the class.
 1. Distribute the buttons so each student has one.
 2. Pair students with different buttons.
 3. Explain the educational objective again.
 4. Students complete their diagrams and conference with another student pair to discuss diagrams.
 5. Students write their paragraphs.
 6. Each student pair conferences with another student pair to review paragraphs. (Add formal teacher conference, if desired.)
 7. Students revise and rewrite their final drafts.
 8. Student pairs read their paragraphs aloud to the class.
 9. Paragraphs with attached buttons are displayed on the classroom walls.

REINFORCEMENT: Send an explanatory letter home describing the use of the Venn diagram for comparing and contrasting. Enclose a sample diagram and encourage each family to use it for a comparing-and-

contrasting activity, such as comparing different breakfast cereals, different soups, different cars, etc.

OTHER BOOKS: Other Caldecotts appropriate for comparing-contrasting activities include *Goldilocks and the Three Bears, Alexander and the Wind-Up Mouse, Fables, The Talking Eggs*, and *Mufaro's Beautiful Daughters*.

"A Swim"

Step 1: Say to students, "Today's story is about swimming. Tell me about a time you've gone swimming."

Steps 2, 3, and 4: Spike It. Ask, "When I say, 'Swimming is...,' what words can you think of to complete the sentence?" Record their answers and continue to probe. Then introduce the book's front matter and ask for predictions.

Steps 5 and 6: Read the story dramatically. Ask students to react to the story and then check predictions.

Step 7: As you read the book together as a group, note the repetition of several words and phrases such as *bathing suit* and *laughed*. Ask students to give the story a different title. Ask students what they think Toad is feeling at the end of the story.

Structure Recognition

Steps 1 and 2: Reread the story using cloze procedures and ask students to circle words on the Spike It list that also appear in the book. Then have students choose words from the Spike It list, first for the Wall of Words, then for their learning logs.

Step 3: "A Swim" has a cause-effect story structure. To demon-

strate this story structure to the students, complete the following activity or one similar to it:

- Pour water from a glass over a sheet of writing paper.
- Ask students what effect the water had on the paper.
- Record on the board:
      Effect: wet paper
- Ask students what caused the paper to get wet.
      Effect: wet paper   Cause: water from glass

Next, mop up the remaining water with a paper towel.
- Ask students, "What effect did my actions have on the paper towel?"
- Record on the board:
      Effect: water-soaked paper,
        changed texture, rips in paper
- Ask students, "What caused the changes in the paper towel?"
- Record on the board:
      Effect: water-soaked paper,   Cause: water
        changed texture, rips in paper

Next, ask students, "What effect did Toad's bathing suit have on the other animals?"
- Record: Effect: laughter

Finally, ask students, "What caused the animals to laugh?"
- Record: Cause: Toad's bathing suit

Step 4: As you reread the book, you may wish to do some of the following:

- Ask students to contrast how Frog and Toad swam.
- Note that none of the animals have "people" names. Have students give the animals names. Use these names when the story is reread. Does using names change the story's language cadence (rhythm)? Do the names add to the story or detract?
- Ask students to write a moral to the story.

Step 5: Have students take turns telling the story as a group or creating an original story called "The Swimming Party."

Language Immersion

SENTENCE LINE-UP

MATERIALS NEEDED: sentences, including all punctuation marks, copied from the story onto sentence strips, which are then cut apart and put into "sentence bags."

OBJECTIVE: When given the individual words and punctuation marks of a sentence from "A Swim," students, working in groups, will rearrange the words and marks into a meaningful sentence and then compare their sentence with the original.

1. Select sentences from the story whose word count, including punctuation marks, corresponds with the number of students you wish to assign to each group. For example, 15 students could be grouped if the following sentence is used: "I will go behind these rocks and put on my bathing suit." (Twelve words, two quotation marks, and one period)

2. Print the sentences on strips and separate the words and punctuation marks. Place the pieces in sentence bags.

3. Arrange students into groups and hand each group a sentence bag.

4. Students arrange the words and marks into a sentence, using the floor or large tables.

5. After the sentence is arranged, students compare the sentence with the original. (The original sentence should be printed on a small strip of paper and placed inside the bag.)

Note: As a variation of this activity, have groups combine the words from the sentence bags and see how many original sentences they can create using as many words and marks as possible.

REINFORCEMENT: Send a sentence line-up activity home in a small paper bag along with an explanation of what it is, how to do it, and why the activity is important. (Have parent helpers prepare the bags.)

OTHER BOOKS: Almost any Caldecott book lends itself to the above activity.

"The Letter"

Step 1: Say to students, "Today's story is about a letter. Tell me about a time you've either written or received a letter or a card."

Steps 2, 3, and 4: Spike It. Ask students, "When I say, 'A letter is...,' what words can you think of to complete the sentence?" Record their answers and continue to probe. Then introduce the book's front matter and ask for predictions.

Steps 5 and 6: Read the story dramatically. Ask students to react to the story and then check predictions.

Step 7: As you read the book together as a group, help students with the words *porch, unhappy*, and *envelope*. Ask students to describe the different emotions of the characters throughout the story. Note the two *t*'s in *matter* and *letter* and the compound word *mailbox*. Ask students why it took the snail so long to deliver the letter. Finally, ask students to predict how long they think it would have taken had a rabbit or squirrel delivered the letter.

Structure Recognition

Steps 1 and 2: Reread the story using cloze procedures and ask students to circle words on the Spike It list that also appear in the book. Then have students choose words from the Spike It list, first for the Wall of Words, then for their learning logs.

Step 3: "The Letter" is an example of the problem-solution story structure. To demonstrate this structure to students, complete the following activity or one similar to it. Say, "I want to write a letter to my cousins, but I don't know how to write a letter. What is my problem, and how can I solve it?" Record on the board the students' responses. Your chart may look similar to the one below:

The Problem Is: I want to write a letter but don't know how

Some Solutions Are: ask someone to help, look in books to see how a letter is written, look at mail from home

The Solution I Choose: ask a friend to help me write a letter; we look in a book for an example

I Do the Solution: my friend and I write a letter

My Reasons for Choosing This Solution Are: answers will vary

Finally, ask students, "What was Toad's problem that made him sad? What was Frog's solution to Toad's problem?"

Step 4: As you reread the story, you may wish to do some of the following:

◆ Practice words with the long *a* sound, such as *snail* and *mail*.
◆ Practice words with the long *e* sound, such as *please*.
◆ Practice words with the *ou* sound found in *house*.
◆ Note the use of *four* and *for*. Find other examples of homophones.
◆ Write Frog's letter on chart paper in proper form. Next, ask students to identify the beginning words (salutation), the words in the message (body), and the ending words (closure). Display the letter.

Step 5: Pass an envelope addressed to Toad around the class as the story is retold. Next, pass an unaddressed envelope around and ask students the following questions: "If you could get a letter right now, from whom would you want it to be? Or if you could send a letter right now, to whom would you sent it?"

Language Immersion

MATERIALS NEEDED: unaddressed envelopes and several examples of friendly letters with addressed envelopes. (For your display examples, you may wish to have letters written by story characters. For example, if the class has read *Strega Nona*, write a letter as if Strega Nona had written to tell the class to pay attention in school and to clean their plates at lunch. Writing the example

letters and envelopes will be time-consuming for you, but they will be letter examples your students won't forget!)

OBJECTIVE: Students will write a friendly letter to Frog or Toad. Students will also address an envelope to accompany the letter.

1. Students select a character to write to.

2. Students examine the example letters and identify all the common format characteristics as well as the letter's language usage and tone. Students also examine Frog's letter to Toad, which is displayed on chart paper.

3. Students write their letters and sample envelopes.

4. Students conference with one another to review one another's letter and envelope. (Add formal teacher conferences, if desired.)

5. Students revise and rewrite their letters. Students make any corrections on their envelopes.

6. Students who wish may read their letter aloud to the class.

7. Teacher "mails" the letters.

8. A letter from Frog and Toad arrives for the class within the next few days and is read aloud to the class.

Note: If possible, get parent helpers to write individual letters of reply to each student and place them in student mailboxes.

REINFORCEMENT: Send a letter home encouraging parents to write letters to their child and have the child write back. Also encourage parents to have their child write letters to relatives, friends, neighbors, etc.

OTHER BOOKS: Other Caldecott books appropriate for the above activity include *Hey, Al, The Relatives Came, The Polar Express, Hide and Seek Fog, Anatole and the Cat, Frog Went A-Courtin',* and *Where the Wild Things Are.*

"The Story"

Step 1: Say to students, "Today's story is about telling a story. Tell me about a time when someone told you a story or you had to make up a story for someone else."

Steps 2, 3, and 4: Spike It. Ask students, "When I say, 'A story is...,' what words can you think of to complete the sentence?" Record their answers and continue to probe. Then introduce the book's front matter and ask for predictions.

Steps 5 and 6: Read the story dramatically. Ask students to react to the story and then check predictions.

Step 7: As you read the book together as a group, ask students to describe how they would feel if they were Frog and were feeling "very green even for a frog." Ask students to suggest other methods Toad might have used to help him think of a story. Record these suggestions for future use during language immersion.

Structure Recognition

Steps 1 and 2: Reread the book using cloze procedures and ask students to circle words on the Spike It list that also appear in the book. Then have students choose words from the Spike It list, first for the Wall of Words, then for their learning logs.

Step 3: "The Story" is based on the sequence-of-events story structure. To demonstrate this structure to students, complete the following activity or one similar to it:

◆ Ask students to watch you move from one place to another around the room. Explain that they will have to recall your movements and to note the order in which you moved from place to place.

◆ Walk to four different points in the room.

- Ask students to recall your movements. Record these on the board using *first, next, then,* and *finally* for sequencing purposes.
- Explain that what has been recorded is a sequence of events that details your movements around the room.
- Finally, ask students to recall the events in "The Story."
- List the events in the story in sequence, using *first, next,* etc.
- Read the sequence of events aloud as a large group.

Step 4: As you reread the story, you may wish to do some of the following:

- Note the verb usage in sequential sentences, such as "stood...standing," "poured...pouring," and "thought...think." Have students practice verb usage by writing pairs of sentences with different verb combinations.
- Note the repetitive use of the sentence "But he could not think of a story to tell Frog" and the repetitive use of *then.* Draw a pictorial story map that sequences the things Toad does to help him think of a story. Connect the events using the repetitive sentence. Display the map.

Step 5: Have students act out the story as they retell it.

Language Immersion

MATERIALS NEEDED: art supplies (optional).

OBJECTIVE: Each student will create an SWBS chart and write an original story based on the Frog and Toad characters.

1. As a large group, students describe the characters of Frog and Toad. (Use Spike It to record the students' ideas.)
2. As a large group, students answer the question "What if Frog and Toad...?" (Record these ideas using Spike It.)
3. Explain the educational objective to students. As a large group, create an SWBS chart for an original Frog and Toad story.
4. Students create their own SWBS charts for their stories. (Stu-

dents who are not able to create an SWBS chart or are unhappy with their own may use the class chart.)

5. Students write the first drafts of their stories.

6. Students conference, first in pairs and then in fours. (Add formal teacher conferences, if desired.)

7. Students revise and rewrite stories.

8. (Optional) Students illustrate their stories and create small books.

9. Stories are recorded on audiotape and placed in the listening library along with the books.

REINFORCEMENT: Introduce parents to SWBS by sending home a letter explaining its function. Encourage parents to create an SWBS chart and fill it out after they and their child have watched a TV program or read a book. Enclose a blank SWBS chart for family use.

OTHER BOOKS: Almost any Caldecott book is suitable for the above activity. Some suggested titles, however, are *Song and Dance Man, The Boy of the Three-Year Nap, The Girl Who Loved Wild Horses, The Steadfast Tin Soldier, Where the Wild Things Are*, and *The Emperor and the Kite*.

A Chair for My Mother

Crow Boy

A Chair for My Mother

Saving money isn't easy, but the warm, loving family in Vera B. Williams's *A Chair for My Mother* decides upon a goal after all their possessions are destroyed in a fire. The goal? To save enough money to buy "a wonderful, beautiful, fat, soft armchair"—a chair for the narrator's mother.

After reading the story, students plan, organize, and create a menu for the Blue Tile Diner, the restaurant where the narrator's mother works. Students also help the family look for furniture stores when they plan, organize, and create a furniture-store ad for the telephone yellow pages.

Book Introduction

Step 1: Say to students, "Today's story is about saving money and buying an armchair. Tell me about a time you've spent money buying something or were with someone who spent money buying something."

Step 2: Spike It. Ask, "When I say, 'Money is...,' what word can you use to complete the sentence?"

◆ Make sure you probe students' responses. For example, when you get the response "Money is used to buy food," continue to probe until you get "restaurant." Then, continue to probe until students supply a list of menu items. (The list will be useful during language immersion.)

Steps 3, 4, 5, and 6: Record their answers. Then introduce the book's front matter and ask for predictions.

Read the book dramatically. Ask students to react to the book and then check predictions.

Step 7: As you read the book together as a group, ask students to define the terms *tips* and *pumps* as they are used in the story. Also, ask

students what the expressions *wash the salts and peppers and fill the ketchups, take a load off my feet*, and *she puts by the savings* mean. In addition, write a list of everything the neighbors gave the family for their new apartment. Finally, you may also want to ask students the following questions:

- "How do you think the family felt when their possessions were destroyed in the fire? How would you feel if you lost all your things in a fire?"
- "Name some possible causes of the fire."
- "If you are caught in a house or apartment that catches fire, what should you do?"
- "How do you know the girl and her mother love each other very much?"

Structure Recognition

Steps 1 and 2: Reread the book using cloze procedures and ask students to circle words on the Spike It list that also appear in the book. Have students choose words from the Spike It list, first for the Wall of Words, then for their learning logs.

Step 3: *A Chair for My Mother* has a problem-solution story structure. To demonstrate this structure, complete the following activity or one similar to it.

Explain that the students will be helping you solve a problem. Say, "Pretend I am your age and I want to buy a present for my mother's birthday, which is three weeks away. I don't want to ask her for money since the present is for her and it's a surprise. What's my problem, and how can I solve it?" Record the students' responses. Below is a sample chart:

| The Problem Is: | I want to buy a surprise birthday gift for my mother, but I don't have any money |
| Some Solutions Are: | save my allowance, ask for an advance on my allowance, run errands/do extra chores for |

	money, ask my dad for money, ask relatives for money, get a job, collect aluminum cans or soda-pop bottles, steal the money
I Choose a Solution:	ask for an advance on my allowance and do extra chores for money
I Do the Solution:	I ask my father for an advance on my allowance and earn extra money by helping him clean the garage
My Reasons for Choosing This Solution Are:	answers will vary

Finally, ask students, "What was the problem in *A Chair for My Mother* and how was it solved?" Record the students' response on chart paper and display it.

Step 4: As you reread the story, you may wish to do some of the following:

◆ Find all the *r* blends of *br, cr, ar, gr, pr,* and *tr.*

◆ Find words that have the *r* after a vowel, as in *purse.*

◆ Have students describe the chair the family buys and reread the description the girl gives in the story: "wonderful, beautiful, fat, soft armchair." Next, give each student a picture of a chair cut from a magazine or old catalog and have each write a sentence describing the chair.

◆ Note how the words *sat* and *set* are used in the story. Practice writing sentences using the two words correctly.

◆ Give students play money and ask them to pretend they are at the Blue Tile Diner. Have students pair off and take turns paying their lunch "bills" with play money.

◆ Design appropriate math problems for your students. For example, find out the average salary of waiters and waitresses working in your area. (Call your local Job Service office.) Use this amount to calculate how long it would take a waitress or waiter to save $200 for a chair if he or she saved half of each week's paycheck. (Students

will be astounded at the number of hours people must work in order to buy things!) Try different hourly wage amounts or salaries and compute how long a person must work in order to buy, for example, a pair of "good" tennis shoes.

Step 5: An alternative to retelling the story is to ask each student to complete the following sentence: "If I lost all of my possessions in a fire, the first thing I would buy would be..."

Language Immersion

MENU MADNESS!

MATERIALS NEEDED: a variety of restaurant menus (ask some restaurants for their children's menus printed on paper placemats, others for their carry-out menus), telephone books with yellow-page listings (find out when the new telephone books will be issued in your area and ask parents, teachers, friends, and businesses to save their old books for you; write a letter to the telephone company requesting old telephone books), art supplies.

OBJECTIVE: After reading different menus, students will plan, organize, and create a menu for the Blue Tile Diner.

1. Distribute menus to students.

2. As a large group, compare the menus and list the similarities. Some similarities should include:
- Each menu item has a name.
- Each menu item has a description (food/ingredient/special preparations).
- Each menu item has a price.
- Most menu items are grouped into categories.
- Most menus contain some art, logo, or border.
- All menus identify the name of the restaurant.

3. Have students look at the illustration of the Blue Tile Diner in the book and predict the types of foods they think would appear on the diner's menu. List the foods on chart paper and display the list.

4. Explain the educational objective.

5. Students group in pairs and plan their menus.

6. Students conference with another pair to review menus.

7. Students revise and rewrite menus.

8. In pairs, students organize and create their menus, using art supplies.

9. As a large group, students exchange their completed menus and "order" from one another's menus.

10. Also as a large group, students explain what they liked about one another's menus and what they would order from each.

11. Menus are displayed around a colorful Blue Tile Diner banner.

Reinforcement: Send a letter home encouraging parents to let their child read the menu aloud to them the next time they eat in a restaurant.

Other Books: Other Caldecotts appropriate for planning menus include *Strega Nona, May I Bring a Friend?, Mice Twice,* and *Frog Went A-Courtin'.*

CALLING ALL YELLOW-PAGE ADS

Objectives: After examining different display advertisements in the yellow pages of a telephone book, students will plan, organize, and create a yellow-page display advertisement for a furniture store.

1. Distribute telephone books.

2. Ask students to identify the various parts of the telephone book and the kinds of information the telephone book supplies. Record this information on chart paper and display.

3. Pose problems to students such as the following:

- Find the area code of a distant state.

- Explain the directions for placing an operator-assisted call.

- Tell the name, address, and telephone number of a restaurant.

- Use the map to locate city hall or a park.

- Find the telephone number of a post office.

- List the emergency numbers for police, fire, and ambulance.

- Find their own telephone number if it's listed.

4. Open the telephone books to the yellow pages. Point out several

examples of display ads (large illustrated ads).

5. Find the furniture-store display ads. Ask students to compare the ads and list the similarities. Some similarities in the ads will include:

- Name, address, and telephone number of the store
- A border, illustration, or art
- Hours the store is open
- Services and brands available

6. Explain the educational objective.

7. Students divide into pairs and plan their ads.

8. Students write and organize their ads.

9. Students conference with another pair and review one another's ads. (Add formal teacher conferences, if desired.)

10. Students revise and rewrite their ads.

11. Students create their ads using art supplies.

12. Pairs regroup into groups of four and share ads.

13. Student groups report to the entire class what they liked about one another's ads.

14. Ads are displayed on the classroom walls.

REINFORCEMENT: Send a letter home encouraging parents to have their child use the phone book whenever the family needs information, such as looking up the phone number when ordering a pizza or finding out the store hours in a display ad in the yellow pages.

OTHER BOOKS: Other Caldecotts appropriate for the creation of display ads include *Anatole and the Cat* (a cat-catching service), *Ben's Trumpet* (trumpet lessons), *The Little House* (house-moving service), and *Fish for Supper* (boats for rent and bait for sale).

Crow Boy

All your students will be able to identify, at least in some small way, with the main character in Taro Yashima's *Crow Boy*. This sensitive, moving story is about a Japanese boy named Chibi who is ridiculed and isolated by his classmates until a new teacher helps him "shine."

In addition to reading the story, students write and illustrate their autobiographies, as well as research a specific topic and write a factual paragraph.

Book Introduction

Step 1: Say to students, "Today's story is about a Japanese boy and the teacher who helped him. Tell me about a time a teacher has helped you."

Steps 2, 3, and 4: Spike It. Ask, "When I say, 'A teacher is...,' what words can you use to complete the sentence?" Record their answers and continue to probe. Then introduce the book's front matter and ask for predictions.

Steps 5 and 6: Introduce the story, using Japanese music in the background. Also, show students where Japan is located on a world map. Ask students to react to the story and then check predictions.

Step 7: As you read the book together as a group, help students with the words *forlorn* and *trudging*. Ask what the expression *kill time* means. Ask students the following questions:

◆   "Why do you suppose Chibi was afraid of the teacher and the other children when he began school?"
◆   "How was Chibi 'different' from the other children at school? What do you suppose was the cause of Chibi's being 'different'?"
◆   "Name some things Chibi knew a lot about. How do you suppose he

learned all those things?"

♦ "What do you suppose Mr. Isobe and Chibi talked about during their private talks together?"

♦ "What effect did Mr. Isobe have on Chibi?"

♦ "What finally caused Chibi to gain respect for himself and from others?"

Structure Recognition

Steps 1 and 2: Reread the book using cloze procedures and ask students to circle words on the Spike It list that also appear in the book. Then have students choose words from the Spike It list, first for the Wall of Words, then for their learning logs.

Step 3: To help demonstrate the sequence-of-events story structure and also provide a learning basis for one of the language-immersion activities, complete the following activity or one similar to it. Explain to students that you are going to put in order—or sequence—events that have happened in your life. In other words, you are going to "chronicle" your life. Ask students to name some things that should be included in a list of events that record or "chronicle" someone's life. Some suggestions might include the following:

♦ Birth date and place
♦ Where and when attended school(s)
♦ Serious illnesses/accidents
♦ Special events (games, birthdays, vacations, meeting famous people)
♦ Family moves
♦ Family members (new sisters, brothers, etc.)
♦ Marriage and children
♦ Jobs

(Retain this list for use during the language-immersion activity.)

Record on chart paper a brief chronicle of your life using the categories students provided. Explain that the completed list is a

sequence of life events.

Next, have students chronicle Chibi's life by inventing a past and future for him. (This is storytelling.) Remind students, however, that their invented past and future must be consistent with what they already know about Chibi from the book.

Step 4: As you reread the book, you may wish to do some of the following:

◆ Ask students to contrast their regular lunch with Chibi's regular lunch.

◆ Have students imitate the different voices of crows as Chibi did.

◆ Ask students to think about a time someone called them a name. Tell students that they are not to share their stories with anyone, just think about them quietly for a while. Next, have students write one word on a slip of paper that tells how they felt when someone called them a name. Do not have students sign their names. Collect the pieces of paper in a paper bag. Draw the pieces of paper out of the bag, one at a time, and read them aloud. Then attach or record each one on a poster that has the words "When you call someone a name, it makes that person feel..." After you've created the poster, ask students why they should not call one another names. Display the poster.

Step 5: Instead of retelling the story, display the life events students created for Chibi and have them tell his "life story" or pick out a life event and have students invent a story about it.

Language Immersion

THIS IS YOUR LIFE!

MATERIALS NEEDED: art supplies, resource materials on birds.

OBJECTIVE: Students will write and illustrate their autobiographies.

1. Using the categories supplied during structure recognition, students will list in order the events to include in their own autobiographies.

2. Each student writes a first draft.

3. Each student conferences with another student and then in groups of four. (Add formal teacher conference, if desired.)

4. Each student revises and rewrites.

5. Each student identifies the number of illustrations to include in his or her autobiography and divides the story into pages.

6. Each student completes the illustrations.

7. Each student compiles illustrations and story text. Cardboard or paper covers may be added.

8. Students who wish may read their books aloud to the class.

Note: If possible, this activity should be completed over the course of a few weeks. You can ask parent helpers to word-process or type each student's story text and provide special wallpaper or cloth covers if you wish to make this an extra-special project. Gluing a school photo of each child on the cover of the book is a nice touch also.

REINFORCEMENT: Send a letter home explaining to parents that their child is writing his or her autobiography. Encourage parents to help their child with dates, spelling of names, etc. Also encourage parents to relate any special childhood stories that their child might wish to include.

OTHER BOOKS: Other Caldecotts appropriate for the above activity include *Bill Peet: An Autobiography, When I Was Young in the Mountains, Owl Moon, Madeline,* and *Madeline's Rescue.*

JUST THE FACTS!

OBJECTIVE: Students will select a bird to study, then read, draw a picture, and write a factual paragraph about it and, finally, briefly summarize their paragraphs aloud for the class.

    1. Model the educational objective by showing a picture of a bird that you have drawn. (If you are not artistic, then so be it. Some of your students won't be either!) A short paragraph describing the bird, its habitat, etc., should be underneath the drawing. Briefly summarize your paragraph aloud for the class. Finally, explain the educational objective to students, linking it to the model you've just presented.

2. After a review of different resource materials, each student selects a bird to research.

3. Students gather facts about their birds, such as description, voice, habitat, and nesting and migration patterns.

4. Students write their factual paragraphs. Upon completion, students conference with one another and then revise and rewrite. (Add formal teacher conferences, if desired.)

5. Students create drawings of their birds.

6. Students attach their paragraphs to their drawings.

7. Students summarize their paragraphs orally for the class.

8. Posters are displayed around the room.

Note: If possible, follow up this activity with a trip to a zoo or with a bird-watching excursion on a nature trail.

REINFORCEMENT: Send a letter home encouraging parents to assist their child in reading factual information by checking out magazines from the local library. Enclose a list of magazines that includes such titles as *Ranger Rick* and *Our Big Backyard.*

OTHER BOOKS: Other Caldecotts that lend themselves to factual paragraph writing include *The Glorious Flight: Across the Channel with Louis Blériot, The Village of Round and Square Houses, Time of Wonder, Castle, Cathedral, You Can Write Chinese,* and *The Thanksgiving Story.*

Jumanji

Ox-Cart Man

Lon Po Po

Jumanji

A
uthor-illustrator Chris Van Allsburg's *Jumanji* is a "thriller-chiller" that your students will find more exciting than a roller-coaster ride! It's a book students DON'T DARE put down! However, when they finally do, they'll practice following directions by creating their own set of game rules and write a newspaper story utilizing the 5W + H news-story format.

Book Introduction

Step 1: Say to students, "Today's story is about playing a game. Tell me about a time when you've played a game."

Steps 2, 3, and 4: Spike It. Say, "When I say the words 'Games are...,' what words can you use to complete the sentence?" Record their answers and continue to probe. Then introduce the book's front matter and ask for predictions.

Steps 5 and 6: This book is VERY dramatic and suspenseful. Use all the dramatics you can muster to make the book come alive. Ask students to react to the book and then check predictions.

Step 7: As you reread the book as a group, help students with words such as *monsoon, tsetse, molten lava, wriggling, slouched*, and *tremendous*. Ask students to act out sentences, such as "She had a look of absolute horror on her face." Ask students to give synonyms for words such as *tremendous* and *peered*. Stop and have students look up *tsetse* and *monsoon* in children's encyclopedias and read the descriptions and definitions aloud. Ask students the following questions:

- "What is opera?"
- "What did Danny and Walter Budwing really take from the park?"
- "Imagine you are peeking through the window at Danny and Walter

Budwing's house and they are playing Jumanji. What are you seeing?"

   ❧   "Explain how the illustrations add to the story."

   ◆   "Which game direction was the most important one to follow?"

Structure Recognition

Steps 1 and 2: Reread the book using cloze procedures and ask students to circle words on the Spike It list that also appear in the book. Then have students choose words from the Spike It list, first for the Wall of Words, then for their learning logs.

Step 3: *Jumanji* has a unique problem-solution story structure because the story is based on a problem solution within a problem solution. In other words, Peter and Judy's initial problem is boredom. Their solution is to play the game Jumanji, which in turn creates another problem. Quickly, Peter and Judy realize their only solution to their new problem is to finish the game and whisk it back to the park. Consequently, to help students better understand the problem-solution story structure, complete the following activity or one similar to it: Explain to students that they will be helping you solve a problem. Say, "I recently worked very hard completing an assignment for one of my classes. I spent a lot of time researching the topic and writing and rewriting. When I got the paper back, however, the teacher wrote the following message: 'Although this is well written, you did not follow the directions for the assignment. In the future, please follow directions.' So I did all that work but didn't get a good grade. However, this wasn't the first time a teacher had told me that I hadn't followed directions. What's my problem and how can I avoid making the same mistake in the future?"

Record students' responses. A sample chart is below:

The Problem Is: not following directions on assignments
Some Solutions Are: write directions down; circle the important parts in written directions; when receiving written directions, rewrite them in numbered order; check directions before starting an assignment

144

I Choose a Solution: always write directions down and circle the important steps

I Do the Solution: the next time I get an assignment, I write the directions down and circle the important steps

My Reasons for
Choosing This
Solution Are: answers will vary

Next, ask students, "The story *Jumanji* also involves a problem and a solution. In fact, the story has more than one problem-solution situation. Can you identify the problem solutions in the story?"

Record the students' responses. Display the chart.

Step 4: As you reread the story, you may wish to do some of the following:

◆ Expand on the idea of "bored people." Use the Spike It method with the phrase "Bored people are..."
Next, ask, "Why was the game designed 'for the bored and restless'?"
◆ Van Allsburg uses dynamic verbs in many of his sentences. Have students identify these verbs and practice using them in sentences.
◆ Note the structure in the following sentence and have students write original sentences using the same structure: "Lying on the piano was a lion, staring at Peter and licking his lips."
◆ Note the use of the words *absolute* and *absolutely*. Have students practice writing sentences using both words appropriately.
◆ Ask students, "How does the author create a sense of excitement in the story? What lessons do you think Peter and Judy learned from the game Jumanji?"

Step 5: Brainstorm about all the possible and impossible things that might happen during a jungle adventure. Next, have students stand in a circle. Set a timer for three minutes and begin passing the book around and playing Jumanji. For example, one student may start out with "A herd of charging zebras with pink stripes—move forward three spaces." Then the book is passed to the next person in line, who might say, "I've run out of water—move back one space." Proceed until the book

reaches the end of the line of students and everyone shouts "Jumanji." Of course, if the buzzer goes off before you shout "Jumanji," you've been trapped!

Language Immersion

FOLLOW THE DIRECTIONS!

MATERIALS NEEDED: several examples of game instructions (directions), such as those from Junior Outburst, Chutes and Ladders, etc. (ask students to bring directions from games they own), several copies of newspaper news stories (not feature stories).

OBJECTIVE: Students will compare several examples of game instructions and then plan, organize, and write a set of directions for their own game.

    1. Distribute several examples of game instructions.

    2. Have small groups of students compare the game instructions and list the similarities.

    3. As a large group, students compile a list of qualities or attributes that most game instructions include. For example, most game instructions state:

- The object of the game
- The number of players and suggested age of players
- How to begin play
- How play continues

    4. As a large group, students describe the directions for dodgeball, hide-and-seek, or any other playground game that is popular at school. Record the game's directions on chart paper and display it.

    5. Divide students into small groups and explain the educational objective.

    6. Students either create an original game and write directions for it or create a variation of an existing game and write its directions.

    7. Student groups conference with each other to check the clarity of their game directions. (Add formal teacher conferences, if desired.)

    8. Students revise and rewrite directions as needed.

9. Student-game directions are gathered and copies are made.

10. Student-game directions from each group are distributed. Students read each group's directions and decide whether directions are clear and easy to follow. Suggestions are made for improvement, if necessary.

11. Final drafts of the game directions are displayed on the classroom walls.

Note: Some groups might want to create a game board to accompany their directions. When they're completed, add them to your classroom library.

REINFORCEMENT: Send a letter home encouraging parents to ask their child to read and follow the directions the next time something needs to be baked or assembled. Also, encourage parents to let their child read game directions aloud to the entire family the next time the family plays a board or card game.

OTHER BOOKS: Other Caldecotts that may be appropriate for the above activity include *Five Little Monkeys, In the Forest, Fables*, and *Where the Wild Things Are.*

EXTRA! EXTRA! READ ALL ABOUT IT!

OBJECTIVE: After comparing several news stories, students will write a brief newspaper story based in part on the book *Jumanji*. Students will use the 5W + H format—Who? What? When? Where? Why? and How?

    1. Give each student a newspaper story and a chart listing WHO, WHAT, WHEN, WHERE, WHY, and HOW.

    2. Have students list the headline of the news story at the top of the chart and answer the questions on the chart as follows: Tell WHO the story is about, WHAT the story is about, WHEN the event in the story took place, WHERE the event in the story took place, WHY the event in the story took place, and HOW the event in the story took place. (Note: Not all news stories contain all of these elements because facts as to why and how events happen may still be

developing when the original story is written to meet the newspaper's deadline.)

3. Read a news story aloud. Have students identify the 5W + H elements as a large group.

4. Have students brainstorm possible news-story ideas based on the events in *Jumanji*.

5. Choose one of the events from the brainstorming session and, as a large group, write a brief news story. (Use an overhead projector so rewriting is easily accomplished.)

6. Each student selects another story idea and writes a brief news story following the 5W + H format.

7. Students conference in pairs and then in groups of four to review one another's stories.

8. Students revise and rewrite news stories. (Add formal teacher conferences, if desired.)

9. Students read their stories aloud for the class. As stories are read aloud, record them on audiotape.

10. The stories are then compiled into a news booklet to accompany the previously recorded audiotape and placed in the listening library.

REINFORCEMENT: Send a letter home encouraging parents to have their child read at least one story a day from the newspaper.

OTHER BOOKS: Other Caldecotts appropriate for the above activity include *Rumpelstiltskin, Madeline's Rescue, Strega Nona, Sylvester and the Magic Pebble, The Amazing Bone, Lon Po Po,* and *Little Red Riding Hood.*

Ox-Cart Man

How did people live before department stores, grocery stores, and automobiles? Students find out in Donald Hall's book *Ox-Cart Man*. With its gentle repetition and unique story structure, *Ox-Cart Man* will have students wanting to read it over and over again. Although students get a look at the past, during language-immersion activities students get a very close look at the present when they read and order from catalogs. Students also read seed-package information and directions, plant seeds, and chart their growth.

Book Introduction

Step 1: Say to students, "Today's book is about a man and his family who lived on a farm a long time ago before cars and trucks were available. Let's use our imaginations and think about what it would have been like to live on a farm a long, long time ago when there weren't any cars, trucks, televisions, radios, or telephones. Think. Tell me about what you'd do on this farm. How would you live?"

Steps 2, 3, and 4: Spike It. Ask students, "When I say the words 'A farm is...,' what words can you think of to complete the sentence?" Record their answers and continue to probe. Then introduce the book's front matter and ask for predictions.

Steps 5 and 6: Read the book dramatically. Ask students to react to the book and then check predictions.

Step 7: As you read the book as a group, help students with words such as *embroidery, harbor, shawl*, and *harness*. Also, have students join in on the story's repetitive words and phrases. Have additional resource material available and show pictures of a loom and a spinning wheel. Explain how they are used. Also, have students look up the following words and explain them: *flax, ox*, and *birch*. (Note: The Barlow knife is named after its inventor, an English cutler.) Find Portsmouth, New

Hampshire, on a map. Finally, ask the following questions:

- "In what way do we as readers see an ending in this book before we see a beginning?"
- "Put one modern appliance in the story. How would it change the family's life?"
- "The Ox-Cart Man filled his cart 'with everything they made or grew all year long that was left over.' What does this mean?"
- "How could we use our natural resources better, just like the Ox-Cart Man and his family?"

Structure Recognition

Steps 1 and 2: Reread the book using cloze procedures and ask students to circle words on the Spike It list that also appear in the book. Then have students choose words from the Spike It list, first for the Wall of Words, then for their learning logs.

Step 3: *Ox-Cart Man* is an excellent example of the list-and-sequence story structure. First of all, the story's sequence follows the "yearly life cycle" of the Ox-Cart Man and his family. In addition, the story includes a list of items that the Ox-Cart Man and his family prepare for market. (Note that the story begins with the Ox-Cart Man going to market and then has the reader discover how the farmer gathered and created all of the items for sale.)

To demonstrate the list-and-sequence story structure, complete the following activity or one similar to it.

Explain that the students will be helping you create a "Year in My Life" chart. The purpose of the chart is to describe a sequence of events during a typical year in their lives.

First, have students generate a list of categories of typical yearly events. Your list may include some of the following:

> Celebrate birthday
> School begins and ends
> School vacations

> Family vacations
> Celebrate holidays
> Sports, music, theater seasons begin and end
> Other seasonal or weather-dependent activities begin and
>   end

Next, record the months of the year on chart paper. Using a classroom calendar, discuss each month and record any events that take place during that particular month. After you have discussed each month, your chart may look something like this:

October
> - celebrate Halloween
> - walk in the woods and parks to see the leaves, which
>   have turned different colors

November
> - school vacation
> - celebrate Thanksgiving
> - play in the first snowfall

Of course, the list and sequence you create will reflect your geography and region as well as your students' ethnicity and culture.

Finally, have students create a "Year in My Life" chart for the Ox-Cart Man and his family on which their yearly tasks are recorded on a monthly basis. Ask, "Would you want to have lived during the period of the Ox-Cart Man? Why or why not?"

Step 4: As you reread the story, you may wish to do some of the following:

◆ Practice writing words with *aw* spelling as in *shawl* and the *au* spelling of *daughter*.

◆ Note that the daughter made mittens from wool, which is a natural fiber. Bring in some nonwool mittens and let students read the labels. They may find words like *polyurethane, polyester,* and *acrylic.* Help students look up these words in a standard dictionary. Note the uses of each material. For example, polyurethane is used

in electrical insulation, polyester is used in swimming pools, and acrylic is used in paints, yet all three can be used together to make a pair of weather-resistant mittens. Continue to have students read one another's clothing labels and as a group create a list of "modern" materials. Next, have students read some maple-syrup ingredient labels. They may find words such as *fructose* and *potassium sorbate*. Help students look up these words in resource books and read the definitions. Finally, ask students, "After looking closely at our present-day clothing and food, what generalizations can you make?"

Step 5: While retelling the story, have students follow the "Year in My Life" chart created earlier and identify how the Ox-Cart Man and his family created each of the items he took to market. Begin with the month of October.

Language Immersion

PLACE YOUR ORDERS!

MATERIALS NEEDED: several different catalogs, catalog order forms (you can choose to use one generic order form or the order form that accompanies each catalog), coffee cans or plastic tumblers, planting soil, a variety of packages of seeds, rulers.

OBJECTIVE: After reading and selecting at least three items from a catalog, students will "order" their items by completing a catalog order form.
   1. Distribute catalogs to students.
   2. Using an overhead projector and a catalog order form recreated on a transparency, complete the order form with the students as a large-group activity. (Students supply catalog-item examples from their catalogs.)
   3. Explain the educational objective and distribute blank catalog order forms. (You can create a simplified version of an order form if an uncluttered version is more appropriate for your students.)
   4. Students complete the order forms.

5. Each student exchanges his or her order form and catalog with another student, who checks the form's accuracy.

6. During oral presentations, students tell the class the name of the catalog from which they placed their order, the items they ordered, and the total cost of their complete order.

7. Order forms are displayed on the classroom wall along with copies of various catalog covers.

REINFORCEMENT: Send a letter home encouraging parents to let their child practice filling out forms that come in "junk mail" as well as unused forms from old catalogs, contests, etc.

OTHER BOOKS: Other Caldecotts that are appropriate for the catalog activity include *Mirandy and Brother Wind* (order a new dress for Mirandy and a new suit for Ezel), *The Polar Express* (write Christmas wish lists), *On Market Street* (go shopping for a friend), and *Mr. Rabbit and the Lovely Present* (order a gift for your mother's birthday).

READ, SEED, AND GROW!

OBJECTIVE: After reading the information and directions on a package of seeds, students will plant the seeds and chart their growth.

1. Supply students with different packages of seeds.

2. Have students compare the information and directions on packages in small groups.

3. As a large group, create a chart of the different types of seeds, their special planting instructions, and the maturity date for each. (Try to get seeds with short germination periods. Also, try to get seeds with approximately the same maturation dates, so everyone's seeds will sprout at about the same time.)

4. Have each student plant a few seeds in a small coffee can or plastic tumbler. Students then create a chart for recording the planting date, the date each type of plant first sprouts, and its subsequent growth over a two-week period.

5. Students chart their seeds' progress daily.

6. At the end of the two-week observation period, students use

information on their charts to help them describe briefly their plant's growth to the class.

7. Plants and charts are displayed in the room before being sent home.

REINFORCEMENT: When the plants and charts go home, send a letter explaining the activity and encouraging parents to give the plant a "home" and watch as their child continues to chart its growth.

OTHER BOOKS: Other Caldecott books that are appropriate for the seed planting activity include *The Relatives Came* (plant the relatives' crop), *Saint George and the Dragon* (plant a magic seed to grow the magic tree), and *A Tree Is Nice* (plant a class tree; create a chart of different kinds of trees, select one, organize a fund-raising drive for money, purchase it, plant it, and take turns watering it).

Lon Po Po

Ed Young's *Lon Po Po: A Red-Riding Hood Story from China* is more than a unique twist to a familiar story—it offers dramatic picture-book art that, according to the book's jacket cover, "combines techniques used in ancient Chinese panel art with a powerful contemporary palette of watercolors and pastels...."

After enjoying a new version of a familiar story, students do some comparing and contrasting of different versions of the Little Red Riding Hood story before they try their hand at writing Chinese.

Book Introduction

Step 1: Say to students, "Today's story is like the story of Little Red Riding Hood. Tell me the story of Little Red Riding Hood. Some of the stories may be a little different, so listen carefully and tell me how your story is the same and how it is different from everyone else's story."

Steps 2, 3, and 4: Spike It. Ask students, "When I say the words 'Little Red Riding Hood is...,' what words can you think of to complete the sentence?" Probe for words to describe the wolf. Record their answers. Then introduce the book's front matter and ask for predictions.

Steps 5 and 6: Read the book dramatically. Ask students to react to the book and then check predictions.

Step 7: As you read the book together as a group, help students with words such as *coughed, route, pluck, journey, fetched,* and *disguised.* Also, have students look up the words *hemp* and *awl* and explain their meaning and use in the story. In addition, show students what a ginkgo tree and its fruit look like. Finally, ask students the following questions:

- ◆ "Let's pretend this story took place in our country. What kind of fruit tree could we substitute for the ginkgo tree?"
- ◆ "Explain how the art in this book made you feel."

◆ "Explain why this book is subtitled *A Red-Riding Hood Story*."

Structure Recognition

Steps 1 and 2: Reread the book using cloze procedures and ask students to circle words on the Spike It list that also appear in the book. Then have students choose words from the Spike It list, first for the Wall of Words, then for their learning logs.

Step 3: *Lon Po Po* is based on a problem-solution story structure. To help students recognize this structure, complete the following activity or one similar to it. Explain to the students that they will be helping you solve a problem. Say, "Pretend I'm your age. I've been left with an older cousin who has agreed to stay with me for the evening while my parents go to a movie. My cousin and I decide to make popcorn. While getting the popcorn from the top shelf, she falls and crashes onto the kitchen table before landing on the floor, where she thumps her head. She appears to be unconscious. What is my problem, and how can I solve it?"

Record the students' responses. A sample chart is below:

My Problem Is:	my cousin has injured herself and no adult is around to help
Some Solutions Are:	call my parents at the movie theater, run and get a neighbor, put cushions under my cousin's head for comfort, call the emergency number, call my cousin's parents, cover my cousin with a blanket, put water on my cousin's forehead
I Choose a Solution:	call the emergency number and follow their instructions; while waiting for help, I call my parents and my cousin's parents
I Do the Solution:	if faced with an emergency situation of this nature, I follow the above steps
My Reasons for Choosing This Solution Are:	answers will vary

Finally, ask students, "What problem did the children in *Lon Po Po* have, and what steps did they take to solve it?"

Step 4: As you reread the story, you may wish to do some of the following:

◆ Ask students to give synonyms for the word *cunning*. Record their synonyms on chart paper, leaving room for two additional lists.
◆ Next, give examples of what the wolf DID that was cunning and ask students to explain how the wolf was cunning. List these under the category title ACTIONS. This list should be on the same piece of chart paper as the synonyms for *cunning*.
◆ Then, give examples of what the wolf SAID that was cunning and ask students to explain how the wolf was cunning. List these on the same chart paper under the category title WORDS.
◆ Finally, ask students to summarize how the wolf was cunning.
◆ Using the same technique and steps, have students analyze the word *clever* and explain how Shang was clever.
◆ Have students substitute words for *heart* in the expression *heart-loving*. Some words might include *warm, kind*, and *good*.

Step 5: While they retell the story, you may wish to have students act out certain scenes.

Language Immersion

COMPARING AND CONTRASTING LITTLE RED RIDING HOOD STORIES

MATERIALS NEEDED: a copy of Trina Schart Hyman's *Little Red Riding Hood* and a copy of Kurt Wiese's book *You Can Write Chinese*, art supplies.

OBJECTIVE: Students will compare and contrast Trina Schart Hyman's *Little Red Riding Hood* and Ed Young's *Lon Po Po*. After completing a Venn diagram, students will write a brief paragraph describing the similarities and differences between the stories.

1. As a group, read *Little Red Riding Hood* aloud.
2. Have small groups of students complete a Venn diagram describ-

ing the similarities and differences between *Little Red Riding Hood* and *Lon Po Po*.

3. Complete a class Venn diagram using all the similarities and differences generated during small-group discussion. Display this diagram.

4. Explain the educational objective.

5. Students write a first draft of their brief paragraph describing two or three similarities and two or three differences.

6. Students conference in pairs and then in groups of four. (Add formal teacher conferences, if desired.)

7. Students revise and rewrite their paragraphs.

8. Anyone who wishes to read his or her paragraph aloud may do so. Paragraphs are then displayed on classroom walls around book-jacket drawings of the two stories.

REINFORCEMENT: Send home a list of titles and authors of folktales, fairy tales, and fables. Encourage parents to check these books out of the library if they and their child have not yet read them.

OTHER BOOKS: Other Caldecott books appropriate for the above activity include *Duffy and the Devil, Rumpelstiltskin, Hansel and Gretel, Goldilocks and the Three Bears, Fables, Tom Tit Tot, Once A Mouse..., It Could Always Be Worse, Mufaro's Beautiful Daughters,* and *The Talking Eggs.*

WRITING CHINESE

OBJECTIVE: After reading Kurt Wiese's *You Can Write Chinese*, students will, in pairs, "write Chinese" by creating wall charts that list their favorite Chinese symbols along with each symbol's Chinese name and its English meaning.

    1. Read *You Can Write Chinese* as a large group. Ask students to generalize by asking the following question: "What can you say about many of the Chinese symbols? (One possible answer: The symbols somewhat resemble objects found in nature and the Chinese culture.)

    2. Show the calligraphy on the cover of *Lon Po Po* and ask students

to compare it with the Chinese symbols in *You Can Write Chinese*. Ask students why the title *Lon Po Po* appears as it does on the book cover. (The strokes that make up the letters in the title are similar to the kinds of strokes used to create Chinese symbols.)

3. Have students work in pairs to select five to ten of their favorite Chinese symbols and to create a chart listing each symbol, its Chinese name, and its English meaning.

4. Have students first create their charts on smaller pieces of paper.

5. Student pairs conference with another pair of students.

6. Students revise and correct any errors in their charts.

7. Students transfer the information from their paper chart to a larger chart made of tagboard.

8. Students present their charts to the large group. Charts are displayed on the classroom wall or in a school hallway.

Note: If you have students in your classroom who can help with the lesson, you have classroom teacher aides! If you have students who speak other languages, have them add their words to the chart.

REINFORCEMENT: Encourage parents to help their child gain an even greater appreciation for the symbols used in English (alphabet) by sending a small paper bag home in which you've placed ten different letters. Have each family create as many words as possible from the ten letters and write the words on the outside of the bag. If students wish, they may bring their bags back to school and compare their words with other students'.

OTHER BOOKS: Other Caldecott books appropriate for the above activity include *Moja Means One*, *Jambo Means Hello*, and *When Clay Sings*.

The Snowy Day

———

Truck

The Snowy Day

Many students will understand exactly how Peter feels in Ezra Jack Keats's beautifully simple story *The Snowy Day*. After all, when you're Peter's age, a world covered with snow IS a special place worthy of an entire day devoted to play!

In addition to enjoying a day with Peter, students also plan and execute a weather report and write a sequel to *The Snowy Day* called *Another Snowy Day*.

Book Introduction

Step 1: Say to students, "Today's book is about snow. Tell me about a time you've played in the snow." (Alternative: "Tell me about a time you've seen pictures of snow or have seen snow on television.")

Steps 2, 3, and 4: Spike It. Ask students, "When I say, 'Snow is...,' what words can you think of to complete the sentence?" Record their answers and continue to probe. Then introduce the book's front matter and ask for predictions.

Steps 5 and 6: Read the book dramatically. Ask students to react to the book and then check predictions.

Step 7: As you read the book together, cue predictable words. For example, read with the students, "It covered everything as far as he could..." but let students read and say "see" without you. Continue to cue words throughout the book. You may also wish to ask students the following questions:

- "We know that Peter's feet made a crunching sound when he walked on the snow. Pretend you are a falling snowflake. What sound do you make when you land on the ground?"
- "Give several reasons why snow is good."

♦ "If it snowed purple gumdrops, what kinds of problems would we have?"

♦ "At the end of the story, Peter gets his friend to play in the snow. What do you think they did all day?" (List their answers on chart paper for display during language immersion.)

Structure Recognition

Steps 1 and 2: Reread the book using cloze procedures and ask students to circle words on the Spike It list that also appear in the book. Then have students choose words from the Spike It list, first for the Wall of Words, then for their learning logs and word bags.

Step 3: *The Snowy Day* has a list-and-sequence story structure. To demonstrate this structure, complete the following activity or one similar to it. Tell students, "Pretend you are Peter's friend and he has asked you to go outside and play in the snow. List all the articles of clothing you will need to wear to play in the snow with Peter." Your list may include some or all of the following:

underwear	socks
mittens (gloves)	hat
scarf	pants
snowsuit (coat, snowpants)	shirt
sweater	boots

Next, say, "Pretend you have all these items in front of you. Put them on. I will ask you in what order you put everything on, so try to remember what you put on first, second, third, and so forth." Let students pantomime putting on the clothing. After they have finished, ask them to tell you in what order they put on their clothing. Number the items in sequence. When individual differences occur, reach a consensus.

Summarize: "We have listed the clothing we would need to wear in order to play outside, and we sequenced, or put in order, the items we would put on first, second, and so forth."

Ask students, "Tell me how the story *The Snowy Day* has a list, and

tell me how the story tells you what happens first, second, and so forth."

Step 4: As you reread the story, you may wish to do some of the following:

◆ Have students write words with the *ow* sounds as represented by the words *snow* and *down*.

◆ Have students write *sn* and *sm* words as represented by *snow*, *smacking*, and *smiling*.

◆ Have students write words that have the *j* sound for *g*, like the word *angel*.

◆ Since the book has interesting punctuation, cover up several punctuation marks with stickees and have students predict what punctuation mark was used.

◆ Make an oral recording as you "read" the pictures. To do this:
-Mask the text.
-Have students propose possible sentences.
-Paraphrase the sentences for the students.
-Have students reach a consensus about which paraphrased sentence is most appropriate.
-Turn on an audiotape recorder.
-Have students recite the sentence.
-Turn off the recorder.
-Proceed to the next page in the book and repeat the above steps.
-After all the sentences are recorded, play the tape back as you show the pictures in the book.

Step 5: Since you've already retold the story in Step 4, here's a chance to practice some original storytelling. Explain to the students that they will be creating a story called *The Rainy Day*. Begin the story with the following:

"One spring morning Peter woke up and looked out the window. Rain had fallen during the night. Wet, slick rain and giant, muddy puddles were everywhere, as far as he could see." Let each student add to the story as you go around the circle.

Language Immersion

WEATHER REPORTS

MATERIALS NEEDED: poster with attachable symbols and the descriptive words RAINY, SUNNY, WINDY, SNOWY; video camera recorder with player and monitor.

OBJECTIVE: Each student will present a weather report that will be videotaped. The report will consist of attaching a descriptive word (RAINY, SUNNY, WINDY, SNOWY) and its symbol to a reusable poster and naming an activity that can be done during that type of weather. For example:

> Today is a _____ day.
>   *(Student places word in space provided.)*
> Symbol _____
>   *(Student attaches appropriate symbol.)*
> Student says, "Today is a windy day. It is a good day for flying a kite."

1. Have students generate a list of activities appropriate for each type of weather—rainy, sunny, windy, snowy. Record these activities on chart paper under the proper category title and its symbol.
2. Explain the educational objective.
3. Model the activity for the students by completing a sample weather report.
4. Students practice their reports.
5. Students take turns presenting their weather reports. Students are videotaped.
6. Play the weather-report videotape back for the class.
7. After evaluating the reports (gently and supportively), ask students to generate a list of dos and don'ts for speaking in front of a group and before a video camera. Post the list for future reference.

REINFORCEMENT: Send a letter home encouraging parents to help their child read the weather report in the newspaper each day.

OTHER BOOKS: Other Caldecott books appropriate for the above activity

include *Umbrella, Frog and Toad Are Friends, Owl Moon*, and *The Moon Jumpers*.

ANOTHER SNOWY DAY

OBJECTIVE: Each student will write a story sequel to *The Snowy Day* that describes how Peter and his friend played in the snow the next day. The title could be *Another Snowy Day*. (Remember, this sequel could be from a few words to several sentences long, depending upon your students.)

1. Display and review the list of ideas that students generated in Step 7 of book introduction (what they thought Peter and his friend did all day when they played in the snow).

2. Explain the educational objective.

3. Remind students to have a beginning, middle, and end to their story.

4. Remind students to concentrate on their story ideas and to use invented spelling. They may also scrounge for words from the walls, other books, etc.

5. After each student has written his or her story, he or she reads it to another student. Students may comment on one another's stories and offer suggestions. (Add a formal teacher conference, if desired.)

6. Any changes the student wishes to make are done after the student conferences.

7. Students or the teacher may read the stories aloud for the class.

8. Stories are displayed on the wall around a poster that looks like a book jacket entitled *Another Snowy Day*. (When you take the display down, place each student's story into his or her evaluation folder.)

REINFORCEMENT: Send a letter home encouraging parents to buy their child a lined spiral notebook for story writing. Explain how parents can encourage story writing after reading a story or watching a TV program.

OTHER BOOKS: Other Caldecott books appropriate for the above activity include *Frog and Toad Are Friends, Hey, Al, The Story of Jumping Mouse*, and *Mr. Rabbit and the Lovely Present*.

Truck

How do you impress upon students that they live in a world in which they are surrounded by print? How do you increase their awareness and understanding of environmental print—the signs, symbols, posters, labels, and placards that are used in everyday life? Donald Crews's distinctively illustrated book *Truck* will help.

Students also extend their appreciation, understanding, and application of environmental print when they read and record examples in their school and create some of their own environmental print to use in the classroom.

Book Introduction

Step 1: Say to students, "Today's book is about traveling on the roads and highways and reading all the signs along the way. Tell me about a time you've traveled along a road or highway and looked at all the signs."

Steps 2, 3, and 4: Spike It. Ask students, "When I say the words 'Signs are...,' what words can you think of to complete the sentence?" Record their answers and continue to probe. Then introduce the book's front matter and ask for predictions.

Steps 5 and 6: Obtain a sound-effects record and play traffic noises as you show the pages of the book. Do not make any comments or read any of the print, signs, or symbols. Ask students to react to the book and then check predictions.

Step 7: As you read the book together as a group, have students explain the signs and all other environmental print on each page. Record each sign on chart paper and write its definition next to it. For example,

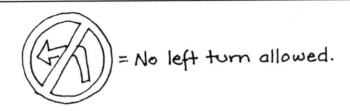

Also, record all environmental print such as TUNNEL AHEAD, LIQUID GAS, and CITY LINE.

You may also want to ask the students the following questions:

◆ "Where do you think the truck started, and where do you think it ended up?"
◆ "What do you think the truck is carrying?"
◆ "Would you like to drive a truck across the country? Why or why not?"
◆ "Name some unusual things trucks might carry."
◆ "What do you think would happen if all the trucks stopped running?"

Structure Recognition

Steps 1 and 2: Reread the book and ask students to circle words on the Spike It list that also appear in the book. Then have students choose words from the Spike It list, first for the Wall of Words, then for their learning logs.

Step 3: *Truck* has a list-and-sequence story structure. To demonstrate it, complete the following activity or one similar to it. Say, "We have many signs, symbols, and posters in the classroom. Name some of the signs, symbols, and posters you see in the FRONT of the room." (Point out what you consider to be the front of the room.)

Next, say, "Now name some of the signs, symbols, and posters you see in the BACK of the room." (Point out the back of the room.)

Finally, say, "Name some of the signs, symbols, and posters you see on the side walls of the room." (Point out the side walls.)

Summarize: "I asked you to list some of the signs, symbols, and

posters around the room. I asked you to list them in sequence or in order starting with the front of the room and continuing to the back of the room until, finally, you named all the signs, symbols, and posters in the room."

Ask students to draw a comparison: "Tell me how the book *Truck* gives you a list of signs, symbols, and posters and puts them in order from beginning to end."

Step 4: As you reread the story, you may wish to do some of following:

- Since most of the signs use all uppercase letters, have students practice printing lower-case letters: *speed limit* instead of *SPEED LIMIT*.
- Have students categorize the signs in the book according to color.
- Introduce other signs such as CAUTION, BUCKLE UP, SLOW. Ask students what color they think these signs should be. (A motor-vehicle booklet will help you think of additional signs.)

Step 5: Have students retell the story from the viewpoint of the tires or the headlights or even the engine.

Language Immersion

PRINT SPRINT!

MATERIALS NEEDED: art supplies, learning logs.

OBJECTIVE: Students will conduct a "walk around the school" during which they will read environmental print and record examples in their learning logs.

1. Explain the educational objective to students.
2. Conduct the walk around the school's hallways, parking lot, playground, etc.
3. Students should record three to five examples of print that they especially like, want to remember, or know how to read.
4. Upon returning to the room, students assemble in small groups and share their examples of environmental print.

5. Students select one example of environmental print to show the class and then explain what it is and where it was (on a fire extinguisher, a step, etc.).

6. Display the examples.

REINFORCEMENT: Send a letter home encouraging parents to point out signs, posters, and labels when driving, shopping, etc. You can even encourage parents to have their child create a sign book while on a long trip.

OTHER BOOKS: Other books appropriate for the above activity include *Ten, Nine, Eight, Alphabetics, Make Way for Ducklings,* and *The Bremen-Town Musicians.*

THIS PRINT'S FOR YOU!

OBJECTIVE: Students will create a sign, poster, or label that can be used in the classroom.

1. To model the educational objective, create a poster, sign, or label for the classroom. Some examples might include:

2. Tell students they are to look around the room and see if anything needs a sign, poster, or label. Next, they are to plan what they want to say on their sign, poster, or label. Then they are to draw it. (If students have difficulty generating ideas, conduct a brainstorming session and encourage them to use some of those ideas.)

3. Students show their sign, poster, or label to another student.

4. Students make any changes on their sign, poster, or label.

5. Individually, students show their sign, poster, or label to the class and then place it in the appropriate spot in the room.

REINFORCEMENT: Send a letter home encouraging parents to play a game where their child puts labels on things in one room in the house (a bedroom, for example). Explain that labels can come down and new labels can be created for a different room in the house.

OTHER BOOKS: Other Caldecotts appropriate for the above activity include *Goldilocks and the Three Bears, Anatole and the Cat, Have You Seen My Duckling?, Ben's Trumpet,* and *The Grey Lady and the Strawberry Snatcher.*

Bibliography

Abrahamson, Richard F. "An Analysis of Children's Favorite Picture Storybooks." *The Reading Teacher* (vol. 34, 1980): pages 167-170.

Armbruster, Bonnie B.; Anderson, Thomas H.; and Ostertage, Joyce. "Teaching Text Structure to Improve Reading and Writing." *The Reading Teacher* (vol. 43, 1989): pages 130-137.

Augustine, Dianne K.; Gruber, Kristin D.; and Hanson, Lynda R. "Cooperation Works!" *Educational Leadership* (vol. 47, 1989-90): pages 4-7.

Barrett, F. L. *A Teacher's Guide to Shared Reading*. Toronto: Scholastic-Tab Publications, 1982.

Barstow, Barbara, and Riggle, Judith. *Beyond Picture Books: A Guide to First Readers*. New York: R. R. Bowker, 1989.

Baskwill, Jane, and Whitman, Paulette. *Whole Language Sourcebook*. Toronto: Scholastic-TAB Publications, 1986.

Baskwill, Jane, and Whitman, Paulette. *Moving On*. Toronto: Scholastic-TAB Publications, 1988.

Baskwill, Jane, and Whitman, Paulette. *Evaluation: Whole Language, Whole Child*. Toronto: Scholastic-TAB Publications, 1988.

Baskwill, Jane, and Whitman, Paulette. *A Guide to Classroom Publishing*. Toronto: Scholastic-TAB Publications, 1986.

Bloom, Benjamin S., et al. *Taxonomy of Educational Objectives: Handbook I: Cognitive Domain*. New York: David McKay Company, 1956.

Bobowski, Rita Cipalla. "The Care and Feeding of Talent." *American Education* (vol. 14, 1976): pages 43-48.

Brandt, R., et al. "On Teaching: A Conversation with Art Costa." *Educational Leadership* (vol. 45, April 1988): pages 10-13.

Briggs, Leslie J. *Instructional Design: Principles and Applications.* Englewood Cliffs, New Jersey: Educational Technology Publications, 1977.

Buncombe, Fran, and Peetoom, Adrian. *Literature-Based Learning: One School's Journey.* New York: Scholastic, 1988.

Butler, Andrea, and Turbill, Jan. *Towards a Reading-Writing Classroom.* Portsmouth, New Hampshire: Heinemann Educational Books, 1984.

Butler, Dorothy. *Cushla and Her Books.* Boston: The Horn Book, 1975.

Calkins, Lucy McCormick. *The Art of Teaching Writing.* Portsmouth, New Hampshire: Heinemann Educational Books, 1986.

Cambourne, Brian. *The Whole Story: Natural Learning and the Acquisition of Literacy in the Classroom.* Auckland: Ashton Scholastic, 1988.

Cambourne, Brian, and Turbill, Jan. *Coping with Chaos.* Portsmouth, New Hampshire: Heinemann Educational Books, 1987.

Cochrane, Orin; Cochrane, Donna; Scalena, Sharen; and Buchana, Ethel. *Reading, Writing and Caring.* Winnipeg: Whole Language Consultants, 1984.

Cohen, S. Alan. *Tests: Marked for Life?* Toronto: Scholastic-TAB Publications, 1988.

Costa, Arthur L., and Lowery, Lawrence F. *Techniques for Teaching Thinking.* Pacific Grove, California: Midwest Publications, 1989.

Costa, A. L., et al. *Developing Minds: Resource for Teaching Thinking,* Alexandria, Virginia: Assn. for Supervision and Curriculum Development, 1985.

Dakos, Kalli. *What's There to Write About?* Toronto: Scholastic-TAB Publications, 1989.

Doake, David B. *Reading Begins at Birth*. Toronto: Scholastic-TAB Publications, 1988.

Dunkel, Harold B. *Herbart and Education*. New York: Random House, 1969.

Dunkel, Harold B. *Herbart and Herbartianism: An Educational Ghost Story*. Chicago: The University of Chicago Press, 1970.

Falkof, Lucille, and Moss, Janet. "When Teachers Tackle Thinking Skills." *Educational Leadership* (vol. 42, 1984): pages 4-9.

Frost, Joan. *Arts, Books and Children: Art Activities Based on Children's Literature*. Omaha: Special Literature Press, 1984.

Gage, N. L., and Berliner, David C. *Educational Psychology*. 3rd ed. Boston: Houghton Mifflin Company, 1984.

Gagne, Robert M,. and Briggs, Leslie. *Principles of Instructional Design*. 2d ed. New York: Holt, Rinehart & Winston, 1987.

Gentry, Richard J. *Spel...Is a Four-Letter Word*. New York: Scholastic-TAB Publications, 1987.

Goodman, Kenneth S.; Smith, E.; Brooks, Meredith; Robert; and Goodman, Yetta M. *Language and Thinking in School: A Whole-Language Curriculum*. New York: Richard C. Owen Publishers, 1987.

Goodman, Kenneth S.; *What's Whole in Whole Language?* Portsmouth, New Hampshire: Heinemann Educational Books, 1986.

Goodman, Kenneth S.; Goodman, Yetta M.; and Hood, Wendy J. *The Whole Language Evaluation Book*. Portsmouth, New Hampshire: Heinemann Educational Books, 1989.

Goodman, Yetta M.; Watson, Dorothy J.; and Burke, Carolyn L. *Reading Miscue Inventory: Alternative Procedures*. New York: Richard C. Owen Publishers, 1987.

Gordon, W.J.J., and Poze, Tony. *Teaching is Listening*. Cambridge, Massachusetts: Porpoise Books, 1972.

Granowsky, Alvin; Middleton, Francis R.; and Mumford Janice. *A Guide for Better Reading*. New York: Scholastic, 1977.

Graves, Michael. *A Word is a Word ...Or is it?* New York: Scholastic, 1985

Groff, Patrick. "An Attack on Basal Readers for the Wrong Reasons." *Arena 1*. Bloomington, Indiana: ERIC Clearinghouse on Reading and Communication Skills, 1989.

Hancock, Joelie, and Hill, Susan. *Literature-Based Reading Programs at Work*. Portsmouth, New Hampshire: Heinemann Educational Books, 1987.

Hart-Hewins, Linda, and Wells, Jan. *Borrow-a-Book: Your Classroom Library Goes Home*. Toronto: Scholastic-TAB Publications, 1988.

Heimlich, Joan E., and Pittelman, Susan D. *Semantic Mapping: Classroom Applications*. Newark, New Jersey: International Reading Association, 1986.

Hillerich, Robert L. *Teaching Children to Write, K-8*. Englewood Cliffs, New Jersey: Prentice-Hall, 1985.

Holdaway, Don. *Stability and Change in Literacy Learning*. Portsmouth, New Hampshire: Heinemann Educational Books, 1984.

Holdaway, Don. *Independence in Reading*. Sydney: Ashton Scholastic, 1980.

Joyce, Bruce, and Weil, Marsha. *Models of Teaching*. Englewood Cliffs, New Jersey: Prentice-Hall, 1986.

Judson, Bay Hallowell. "What is in a Picture?" *Children's Literature in Education* (vol. 26, 1989): pages 181-185.

Kagan, Spencer. "The Structural Approach to Cooperative Learning," *Educational Leadership* (vol. 47, 1989-90): pages 12-15.

Kline, Peter. *The Everyday Genius: Restoring Children's Natural Joy of Learning—and Yours, Too*. Arlington, Virginia: Great Ocean Publishers, 1988.

Labbo, Linda D., and Teale, William H. "Cross-Age Reading: A Strategy for Helping Poor Readers." *The Reading Teacher* (vol. 43, 1990): pages 362-369.

Loughlin, Catherine E., and Martin, Mavis D. *Supporting Literacy*. New York: Columbia University Teachers College Press, 1987.

Lynch, Priscilla. *Using Big Books and Predictable Books*. Toronto: Scholastic-TAB Publications, 1986.

Manning, Maryann Murphy; Manning, Gary L.; Long, Roberta; and Wolfson, Bernice J. *Reading and Writing in the Primary Grades*. Washington, D.C.: National Education Association of the United States, 1987.

Murray, Donald M. *Learning by Teaching*. Portsmouth, New Hampshire: Boynton/Cook Publishers. 1982.

Myers, Miles. *A Procedure for Writing Assessment and Holistic Scoring*. Urbana, Illinois: National Council of Teachers of English, 1980.

Nathan, Ruth; Temple, Frances; Juntenen, Kathleen; and Temple, Charles. *Classroom Strategies that Work: An Elementary Teacher's Guide to Process Writing*. Portsmouth, New Hampshire: Heinemann Educational Books, 1989.

Newman, Judith M. *Whole Language: Theory in Use*. Portsmouth, New Hampshire: Heinemann Educational Books, 1989.

Newman, Judith. *The Craft of Children's Writing*. New York: Scholastic-TAB Publications, 1984.

Ollmann, Hilda E. "Cause and Effect in the Real World." *Journal of Reading* (vol. 33, 1989): pages 224-225.

Pearson, David P., and Johnson, Dale D. *Teaching Reading Comprehension*. New York: Holt, Rinehart & Winston, 1978.

Peetoom, Adrian. *Shared Reading: Safe Risks with Whole Books*. Toronto: Scholastic-TAB Publications, 1986.

Perry, Leslie Anne, and Sagen, Patricia. "Are Basal Readers Becoming Too Difficult for Some Children?" *Reading Improvement* (vol. 26, 1989): pages 181-185.

Pickering, Thomas C. "Whole Language: A New Signal for Expanding Literacy." *Reading Improvement* (vol. 26, 1989): pages 144-149.

Pinnell, Gay Su; Fried, Mary D.; and Estice, Rose Mary. "Reading Recovery: Learning How to Make a Difference." *The Reading Teacher* (vol. 43, 1990): pages 282-295.

Rhodes, Lynn K. "I Can Read! Predictable Books as Resources for Reading and Writing Instruction." *The Reading Teacher* (vol. 38, 1981): pages 511-518.

Routman, Regie. *Transitions From Literature to Literacy*. Portsmouth, New Hampshire: Heinemann Educational Books, 1988.

Rowe, M. B. "Wait Time and Rewards as Instructional Variables: Their Influence on Language, Logic, and Fate Control." *Journal of Research in Science Teaching* (vol. 11, 1974): pages 81-94.

Ruggiero, Vincent Ryan. *Teaching Thinking Across the Curriculum*. New York: Harper and Row, 1987.

Rye, James. *Cloze Procedure and the Teaching of Reading*. London: Heinemann Educational Books, 1982.

Sadow, Marilyn W. "The Use of Story Grammar in the Design of Questions." *The Reading Teacher* (vol. 30, 1982): pages 518-521.

Schlichter, Carol L. "Thinking Skills Instruction for All Classrooms." *Gifted Child Today* (March/April 1988): pages 24-29.

Schlichter, Carol L. "Talents Unlimited: An Inservice Education Model for Teaching Thinking Skills." *Gifted Child Quarterly* (vol. 30, 1986): pages 3-7.

Schlichter, Carol L. "A Model Project: Help Students Become Active Thinkers." *Early Years/K-8* (vol. 15, Jan. 1985): pages 38-40.

Sendak, Maurice. *Caldecott & Co.: Notes on Books & Pictures.* New York: Farrar, Straus, Giroux, 1988.

Slavin, Robert E. *Student Team Learning: An Overview and Practical Guide.* Washington, D.C.: National Education Association, 1983.

Smith, Frank. *Reading Without Nonsense.* New York: Columbia University Teachers College Press, 1979.

Smith, Frank. *Essays Into Literacy.* Portsmouth, New Hampshire: Heinemann Educational Books, 1983.

Soehl, Jolene; O'Brien, Jim; Stensrud, Diane; and Hoogland, Jodi. *Reading Comprehension Presenter Packet.* Davenport, Iowa: Davenport Community Schools, 1987.

Spache, George D. *Good Reading for Poor Readers.* Champaign, Illinois: Garrard Publishing Company, 1978.

Strong, Richard W.; Hanson, J. Robert; and Silver, Harvey F. *Questioning Styles and Strategies: Procedures for Increasing the Depth of Student Thinking.* Moorestown, New Jersey: Hanson Silver Strong and Associates, 1986.

Thompkins, Gail E., and Webeler, MaryBeth. "What Will Happen Next? Using Predictable Books with Young Children." *The Reading Teacher* (vol. 36, 1983): pages 498-503.

Thompson, Gare. *52 Ways to Use Paperbacks in the Classroom.* New York: Scholastic, 1989.

Trachtenburg, Phyllis. "Using Children's Literature to Enhance Phonics Instruction." *The Reading Teacher* (vol. 43, 1990): pages 648-653.

Turbill, Jan. *No Better Way to Teach Writing!* Rozelle, New South Wales: Primary English Teaching Association, 1982.

Turbill, Jan. *Now, We Want to Write!* Rozelle, New South Wales: Primary English Teaching Association, 1983.

Van Hanen, Max. *The Tone of Teaching*. Toronto: Scholastic-TAB Publications, 1986.

Villiers, Una. *Luk Mume Luk Dade I kan Rit*. Toronto: Scholastic-TAB Publications, 1989.

Walshe, R. D. *Children Want to Write!* Donald Graves Association, 1981.

Watson, Dorothy; Burke, Carolyn; and Harste, Jerome. *Whole Language: Inquiring Voices*. Toronto: Scholastic-TAB Publications, 1989.

Weaver, Constance. "The Basalization of America: A Cause for Concern." *Arena 1*. Bloomington, Indiana: ERIC Clearinghouse on Reading and Communication Skills, 1989.

Whaley, Jill Fitzgerald. "Story Grammars and Reading Instruction." *The Reading Teacher* (vol. 34, 1981): pages 762-771.

Photograph by Debra L. Brandt

Christine Boardman Moen fell in love with many of the books in the Caldecott collection as she enjoyed them along with her two children, Alex and Ruth. Now a freelance instructional designer, Christine is a former classroom teacher who also wrote a weekly education column entitled "Today's Challenge" while a Newspaper-in-Education coordinator.

A strong advocate of broad-based literacy education, Christine conducts cross-age reading activities in her children's school and is the writer/editor of *Read On,* a quarterly literacy newsletter published by the Bi-State Literacy Council.

Published in various professional magazines, Christine continues to design instructional materials for classroom presentations, workshops, and conferences.